D0478849

CALGARY PUBLIC LIBRARY

DISCARDED

SOUTHWOOD BRANCH

385. 0941 FRA
Frater, Alexander.
Stopping-train Britain
95483203

STOPPING-TRAIN BRITAIN

A RAILWAY ODYSSEY

SOUTHWOOD BRANCH

020017412.

STOPPING-TRAIN BRITAIN

A RAILWAY ODYSSEY BY
ALEXANDER FRATER

PHOTOGRAPHED BY
ALAIN LE GARSMEUR

HODDER AND STOUGHTON
LONDON   SYDNEY   AUCKLAND   TORONTO

In memory of my father, who would have enjoyed
making these small journeys.

ACKNOWLEDGMENTS

The author and publisher would like to thank the following for permission to reproduce
photographs: Margaret Duff Collection, pp 14 (top), 18; Carlisle Libraries Group, pp 20
(top), 60; *Lancashire Evening Telegraph*, p 25 (top); Collection of N. G. Coates, pp 25
(bottom), 30; *Illustrated London News* Picture Library, pp 27 (top), 158; Lancashire Library,
Hyndburn District, p 27 (bottom); Lancashire Library, Burnley District, p 34; Isaac
Hailwood, p 43; J. W. Armstrong, p 50; R. Sankey, p 62; British Rail, pp 67 (BR/WEH/
4/3/1), 83 (BR/NBR/4/406), 142 (BR/HR/4/32/4), 147 (BR/HR/4/29/11), 149 (BR/HR/
4/29/5); National Railway Museum, pp 70, 75, 76, 154; British Rail/Oxford Publishing
Company, p 90 (top); C. C. Green, pp 94, 95; The National Library of Wales, pp 103, 108,
110, 111; Norfolk Museums Service: Cromer Museum, pp 123, 126; London Borough of
Camden, p 151.

British Library Cataloguing in Publication Data

Frater, Alexander
    Stopping-train Britain.
    1. British Rail   2. Railroads – Great Britain – Branch Lines
    I. Title
    385'.0941   HE3816

ISBN 0 340 32451 1

*Copyright © 1983 by The Observer Ltd. First printed 1983. Second Impression March 1984. All rights reserved. No
part of this publication may be reproduced or transmitted in any form or by any means, electronic or mechanical,
including photocopy, recording, or any information storage and retrieval system, without permission in writing from the
publisher. Printed in Italy for Hodder and Stoughton Limited, Mill Road, Dunton Green, Sevenoaks, Kent. Photoset
by Rowland Phototypesetting Limited, Bury St Edmunds, Suffolk. Hodder and Stoughton Editorial Office: 47
Bedford Square, London WC1B 3DP.*

Contents

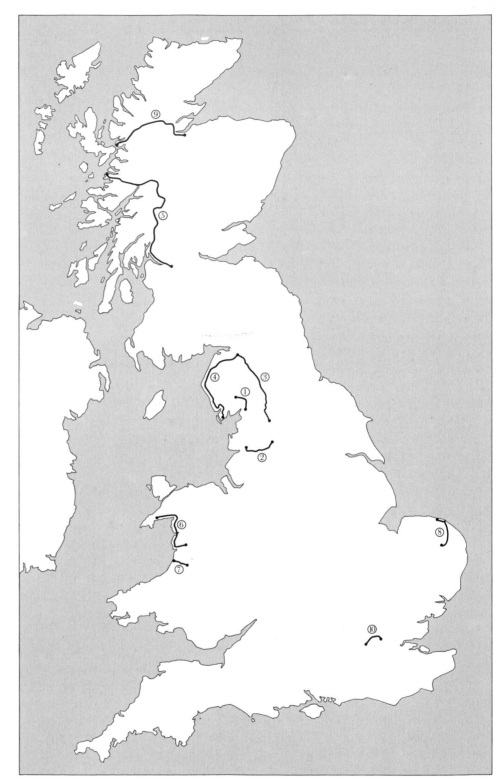

Introduction

When I was invited by the *Observer* Magazine to embark on a series about country trains, I accepted for two reasons. The first was that in my particular trade it is very unwise to say no; Fleet Street editors don't like being turned down, and persistent offenders risk being ordered off to some snake-ridden South American swamp to look for elderly Nazi war criminals. Second, though I had never felt any particular enthusiasm for railways, the phrase 'country trains' had always seemed to me one of the most evocative in the English language, conjuring up images of tracks winding away past stands of oak and fields of barley, of solitary villages with elms in the churchyard and a good batting wicket on the green, of a sparkling morning sky reflected in the waters of some glassy Highland loch, of the harvest being taken in on a still August evening heavy with the promise of thunder. Country trains stood for all that. The values they represented were permanent and reassuring. And while city trains – specially London trains – tended to be squalid, crowded and evil-smelling, with the philosophical musings of some of their passengers ('Doug of the Clock End Kicks to Kill', 'Knife a Nigger Today') thoughtfully inscribed on the carriage walls for others to ponder, country trains remained as wholesome as freshly baked bread. The only note of menace was provided by the wasps coming through the windows in the late weeks of summer to do some low, hard flying around the baskets of passengers transporting newly made jam. Country trains stood for country values, and they were well nigh indestructible.

In the course of my travels I was interested to note how accurate these pastoral clichés turned out to be. The landscapes through which Britain's country trains travel are remarkably diverse and beautiful. Of course there are the boring bits, the dreary housing estates, down-at-heel townships and colonies of caravans, like those that are spawning inexorably along the Welsh coast. And by no means all my fellow passengers turned out to be the apple-cheeked folk, beaming and bucolic, I had anticipated; inevitably I met my share of louts and drunks. But most people, including the rail staff I travelled with, were notably kind and helpful. Over the years, as a London commuter, I had grown accustomed to railwaymen displaying a terrible impatience with human frailty, their standard responses ranging from dumb insolence all the way up to homicidal mania. I had assumed that the same attitudes would prevail out in the country, but the great majority of the drivers, guards, signalmen and station staff with whom I came in contact were

smashing – keen, funny, knowledgeable and anxious that I should appreciate the routes they worked and understand the nature of their duties and responsibilities.

One of the surprising things about them was their affection for trains. Almost to a man they were unashamed enthusiasts, old spotters who had grown up and rallied to the colours; quite a few were following in the footsteps of their fathers and grandfathers, and regarded the railways as a family concern. In many cases their feelings for the ancient conveyances they coaxed and urged over the miles of worn metals were so strong that my lifelong indifference was gradually replaced by a faint, furtive stirring of interest. And the more they talked the more I became aware of the astonishing complexity and richness of railway history, lore and language. It slowly dawned on me that the little diesel rattling along between, say, Shrewsbury and Hereford, is only doing so because for a century and a half generations of engineers have been obsessively solving millions of problems in the cause of a single principle. Every artifact, be it the lock on a level-crossing gate or the driving mechanism of a shunting engine, has been considered, reduced to its most logical elements and then resolved, often with surprising elegance and simplicity.

Travelling about on rural trains is not unlike seeing the country from horseback. One has the same elevated seat and moves at the same comfortable pace. It allows the rider time to observe the landscape, to note everything from the movement of cloud shadows across a moor to butterflies roosting on a twig. The experience taught me something important. Journalists who write the kind of stuff I write tend to assume that the grass on the other side of the fence is always greener, that assignments get better in direct proportion to their distance from home. It has long been my understanding, for example, that to do something worthwhile you needed to visit a place that was really remote and difficult, like Burma or the Siberian hinterlands. But then I undertook this series of small journeys around Britain and began to comprehend what an astonishingly rich and varied country I was travelling through. The people I met had a strong sense of identity and knew a lot about their neighbourhoods. They had good stories to tell. Patagonia? Who needs it? For a writer there are equally rich veins waiting to be worked in East Anglia or the Western Highlands.

The choice of lines in this book is notably eccentric, and the fault for that is mine. I began the project from a position of ignorance which, I am afraid, was maintained almost until the finish. Lacking any sort of master plan, I simply rang around the various regional British Rail press officers and asked about their most interesting and attractive runs, but lines were also selected on the basis of chance conversations with people; the laws of natural progression meant that one journey invariably led to another. For example, I first heard about one of the greatest runs in the kingdom, the classic Settle to Carlisle, while I was sitting in the British Rail press office in Preston, Lancashire. I had called in to pick up some cuttings on the line to Colne but both press officers were at a meeting and, with nothing better to do, I began answering their

OPPOSITE
Loch Carron on the Inverness to Kyle of Lochalsh line.

9

telephones. When a call came through from a local radio station demanding a comment on reports that the Settle to Carlisle line would shortly be closed due to the state of its viaducts I had to own up and admit that I had no idea what he was talking about. But then, impressed by the interviewer's obvious depth of feeling, I assumed the role of questioner instead and was so interested in what he had to say that I made an urgent mental note to try the Settle to Carlisle just as soon as possible.

It is because it was all done on such a casual basis that the collection is so lopsided. Readers may notice that, while much attention has been paid to routes in the North-West of England, there is no reference at all to the celebrated railways of the West Country and lines like the Truro to Falmouth, the Penzance to St Ives. To anyone who feels aggrieved because these – or any other outstanding routes – have been left out, I offer my apologies; we simply ran out of time. Should Alain Le Garsmeur and I ever embark on a sequel we shall endeavour to rectify a few of the more obvious omissions.

The assignment was a remarkably happy one, and great fun to do – though the fact that the country train is clearly a doomed species lent it a certain piquancy. Many rural railmen are convinced that, within a decade or so, they will no longer have trains to operate. They say that circumstances have left the country train in a dangerously vulnerable position. If the pessimists are right then we shall soon see the partial dismantling of the greatest of all our Victorian monuments. The sleepers will be split for fence posts, or firewood, the rails and rolling stock recycled into Fiestas or Type 42 destroyers – and Britain will have lost its most agreeable way of moving around and taking stock of itself.

Perhaps the rot has already set in. I met an Inter-City driver who spoke, with some bitterness, of his declining social status. 'I can remember the days when, at the end of a journey, passengers would walk up the platform and say thank you,' he told me. 'That was quite a normal occurrence. It's very rare now – though occasionally a retired couple, who perhaps remember the way things used to be done, will tap on your window and smile. I'm talking about mainline working, of course. On the small trains you still get human contact, and a lot of the drivers prefer working the country lines for that reason. And also because the pace isn't so hectic.'

Many travellers would agree. Though there is no denying the speed, silence and comfort of the big 125 expresses, the people aboard are not encouraged to wander back for a chat with the guard about crops and the prices fat cattle are fetching at auction. He is a busy, preoccupied man who probably has a thousand tickets to examine, while the driver, hermetically sealed into his cab, is even less accessible. As for the passenger, gazing through those heavy tinted windows, it is difficult for him to believe that he belongs to the same world as, for example, the ploughman briefly glimpsed towing a bright cloud of gulls behind him, or the embankment carpeted with Oxford ragwort, the ubiquitous railway weed which came from the slopes of Vesuvius via – mysteriously – the Oxford Botanic Gardens. These sleek monsters howling along with a noise like a succession of Atlantic gales enjoy only the most ephemeral contact with the landscapes through which they are passing.

And it is hard to imagine them being responsible for the remarkable literary output that the older, smaller trains inspired. *Adelstrop* was, admittedly, seen from an express which 'drew up there/Unwontedly' one lovely afternoon in late June. But the heavy soundproofing in today's express carriages would have prevented Edward Thomas from hearing that immortal blackbird 'Close by, and round him, mistier,/Farther and farther, all the birds/Of Oxfordshire and Gloucestershire' while he might well have been so furiously preoccupied by his inability to remove the cellophane wrapper from his British Rail sandwich that he wouldn't have noticed where the train had stopped anyway. And it was a sleepy country service of which Siegfried Sassoon wrote, in *Memoirs of a Fox-hunting Man*, 'Ten minutes late, in the hot evening sunshine, my train bustled contentedly along between orchards and hop gardens, jolted past the signal-box, puffed importantly under the bridge, and slowed up at Baldock Wood.' When the country trains have finally gone, that, I suspect, is how many of us will choose to remember them – last survivors of an age of innocence.

My thanks are due to all the railwaymen who helped me on my way and answered my questions with such tolerance and good humour, but most particularly to Peter Crookston, sometime editor of the *Observer* Magazine, whose idea the series was.

Last line to the Lakes

OXENHOLME TO WINDERMERE

The line from Oxenholme to Windermere is really a single-track railway laid along a country lane. For 10¼ miles it sinks and rises through the fells, minding its own business, causing no offence, not even frightening the sheep. Yet it is unique among railways in that, before its construction in 1844, it stirred one of the world's greatest poets into such a frenzy of rage that he dashed off a furious – and widely quoted – sonnet called 'On the Projected Kendal and Windermere Railway'. The poet was Wordsworth, and he believed that the tide of trippers it would bring from the Lancashire cotton towns was going to flood his beloved Lake District with drunkenness, litter and working-class debauchery. Wordsworth lost his battle; the Kendal and Windermere Railway Company won it. Today both parties have gone, taking their mutual rancour with them, and the line, peaceful and obscure, blends into the landscape as unobtrusively as an old cattle track.

Oxenholme – *holmr* is Old Norse for 'water-meadow' – is a halt on the main London-to-Glasgow rail route. The high-speed Inter-City services come thundering through the station like a succession of tropical storms, bending and shaking the trees, causing the ancient twin-carriage train tucked away behind the refreshment stall on platform three to rock slightly on its wheels. The station office is fashioned from sandstone and has the air of a prosperous little Lakeland hotel. Lace curtains hang behind the mullioned upstairs windows and, on the grassy hill behind, oaks and beeches stand tricked out – when I was there – in autumn colours so flamboyant that they seemed neon-lit. Every hour or so there is a small flurry of activity around the branch-line siding: the driver and guard board their train, the loudspeaker announces the departure of the service to Windermere (calling at Kendal, Burneside, and Staveley), doors slam behind late passengers and then, diesels straining, it moves off along the single track and vanishes down a slope and into a copse, its passage marked by a banner of blue smoke flapping over the tree-tops.

Four minutes later it approaches Kendal through housing estates and over Long Pool bridge. The station is now derelict and smells of decay, its spacious offices and public rooms slept in by vagrants, its crumbling station-master's house, soaring above the platform like a graceful stone pavilion, used as a squat by flocks of doves. But, until 1972, Kendal was famous among railmen. 'It were the parcels,' says Dick Whiteside, an intense, quietly spoken Oxenholme porter. 'Today that station is a disgrace, but then it were the pride of the district

ABOVE
An Edwardian outing. Members of the Zion Chapel at Kendal station en route to a day in the Lake District.

RIGHT
Kendal station – derelict, smelling of decay, slept in by vagrants.

and the 18.35 Kendal Parcels were a Class One train, pulled by a Jubilee or Royal Scot engine fitted with express headlights. It went up to London at express speeds, seventy miles an hour all the way, and if it were delayed, well the sky fell in. There were no general-purpose Black Five hauling *that*; only the best would do for the Kendal Parcels.'

Fifty men helped prepare the train, which spent the day in the loading bay behind the station. 'An average consignment,' Mr Whiteside recalls, 'would be a thousand cartons from K Shoes, snuff from Illingworth's and Gawith Hoggarth – there were seven snuff mills here once – and carpets from Goodacre's. In the evening the shunt engine brought the train out and when we reported for duty (I were a guard on the Parcels) you'd find everything ready and waiting: tender filled, coal loaded, fire lit. All you had to do were dump your kit aboard and go.'

The proliferation of manufacturing around Kendal, a quiet market town usually associated with the production of mint cake, is due to the passage through it of the River Kent, claimed to be the swiftest stream in the country. So many mills sprang up along its green banks that, midway through the last century, Kendal was more industrialised than Birmingham, the fells loud with the clamorous creak and splash of countless water-wheels. There were textile mills, paper mills, carpet mills, rope mills, snuff mills, gunpowder mills, – processing hazel and ash charcoal from the forests – and bobbin mills. All that produce was carried away by train, and the station became the busiest place in town.

The line leaves Kendal past a junk-yard and the turbulent waters of the Kent, and heads for Burneside and its three crossings. Only the Higher is manned today. Its keeper, Mr T. W. Dixon, is gentle and scholarly-looking, and has spent much of his working life tending rails on the permanent way. He sits in a tiny hut beside the pretty stone cottage, now occupied by a builder of fibreglass canoes, which was once the keeper's residence.

The hut contains a heater, a kettle, a telephone, and The Book. The phone is connected with the instruments installed at the unmanned crossings, and anyone using the crossings is supposed to call Mr Dixon first. Most do, some don't, and, occasionally, there is an incident. 'The last was on Budget Day, March 10,' said Mr Dixon, showing me a picture of a mangled Cortina clipped from the *Westmorland Gazette*. 'That were at Burneside Lower, and this chap were clobbered because he failed to get permission. Mind you, he were lucky; he just got up and walked away from it, more or less.'

Everything using the crossings is neatly recorded in The Book – '11.12: Milk Cart Crossing', '14.36: Dust Cart Crossing' and, twice a day, the passage through his gates of fifty milking cows is noted too. After they have passed, Mr Dixon, a fastidious man, seizes a broom and sweeps his crossing until it's as spotless as a kitchen floor.

At Burneside station the train passes the Cropper paper mill cricket ground, glimpsed through trees, then begins its ascent to Staveley, where the station, unmanned, stands beside the Railway Hotel and in the high, forbidding shadow of Hugill Fell. The village, which once resounded to the clatter of

Mr T. W. Dixon, gentle and scholarly looking, is Keeper of The Book.

The line blends into the landscape as unobtrusively as an old cattle track.

15

bobbin mills, is a neat settlement of cottages built about a small, square-towered church with a fine Burne-Jones window; one of the headmasters of the local school, founded in 1538, was Joseph Martindale, a celebrated authority on mosses. Then the line, heading west, climbs to the brow of the hill and drops quickly down to Windermere. At the station approaches, like a glimpse through a camera shutter, there is a brief view of bright water below. The run takes twenty-five minutes.

One of the three daily trains that used to race all the way up here from Euston was the fashionable 10.50 Lakes Express, patronised by the tycoons and peers who owned holiday homes around the lake and who whiled away the journey over lobster and goblets of chilled Tokay in the dining-car. There were also regular services from Leeds, Liverpool and Manchester Exchange and, on summer Sundays, the Excursion Specials came steaming in like Atlantic convoys. The three-hundred-yard platform that accommodated them swallows the toy train using it today. The spreading tracery of tracks has been torn up for scrap, and so has the vacuum-operated turntable, able to handle any engine in the land – except for the giant Pacifics, so big they had to go back up the line tender-first. Windermere's large staff, which included an industrious band of carriage cleaners, has now dwindled to a couple of porters and a clerk. But the booking hall has retained its classical portico, and flower baskets hang from the platform roof. On the slate walls of the station, stuck up beside the Red Star and Golden Rail ads, are auctioneers' notices advising the sales of

Passengers at Windermere station in 1910 board a charabanc for the run down to the lake.

Gilpin Farm and Low House Farm (228 acres at Long Sleddale). The passengers, many of them foreign tourists, wait patiently, some dozing with folded arms. Bees drone in the sunshine. Butterflies float among the brambles on the derelict trackbed, climbing wildly for cover whenever the train approaches.

In driving terms it's an old man's line, a peaceful, untaxing run through some of the loveliest country in England. Edgar Russell, a white-haired Justice of the Peace (he sits on the Lancaster and Morecambe Bench) has been driving for forty years, learning his craft overseas during the war. Then the army had a complete railways division, founded to get the troops to their battles or bivouacs on time. Mr Russell drove engines in India, Iran, Syria, Italy and the Western desert and, for a youngster who had dreamt of nothing more onerous than taking expresses down to Penzance or Carlisle, it was a tough training ground. 'I used to do runs where you'd start off wearing shorts on the footplate and arrive at your destination in snow boots and goggles. In Persia I worked trains down a line that wound around the inside of a hollowed-out mountain. Back home, I've driven everything, all the big high-speed trains, electric and diesel, all the Inter-Cities. I've even taught other drivers. After all that, this is a lovely branch line to finish your life on. Who wouldn't envy me? I spend my days surrounded by all this wonderful scenery and chatting to some very nice people. You get a decent class of person on this run. Hardly any of the seat-slashing brigade, thank goodness.'

Mr Russell is not at all magisterial but has, rather, the manner of a country churchman or a retired colonial bishop; and I rode with him one fine morning as he took his train up the hill out of Windermere. The aromatic air smelt of juniper and had a bite like cold gin; around us the fells glowed in the soft, butter-coloured light. We clattered to the top of the gradient and passed under the first of the dozen stone bridges crossing the line. 'We call this one the Bridge of Sighs,' said Mr Russell. 'It's not us who sigh, it's these old diesels, and what they give is a sigh of contentment; it's mostly downhill now.' On the journey over he had almost bagged a buzzard. 'It happens when they're trying to pick a rabbit off the line and leave it too late to get out of the way. These local rabbits fight back. I always slow for buzzards, but the greedy ones can get into trouble.'

The line's catalogue of victims includes a number of more sombre entries. Descending briskly towards Staveley, he pointed to another bridge. 'A woman from Ilkley killed herself here a while ago,' he said, as we raced under it. 'We don't know whether she jumped or suddenly stepped out from behind. Either way, it was too late for the driver to do anything and afterwards, as I recall, though they hunted through the woods, they couldn't find one of her arms and one of her legs. It's terrible for the victim, but also very bad for the driver. His nightmares can go on for years.' Local railmen occasionally take their lives on the line, too. 'Our lads sometimes use it for that purpose,' a supervisor had told me sadly the previous day. 'The last one was an Oxenholme porter who thought he had cancer. One afternoon he walked out, without a word, and put his head on the rail as the train came by.'

Windermere's station (with the Station Hotel a comfortable stroll away) soon after completion.

BELOW
Much of the old building has gone. Today only a single platform is operational.

The people who perform the grisly task of clearing up afterwards are the gang of five maintenance men who constantly check the line on foot. They are based at Kendal and, apart from the few distressing occasions when they must liaise with the local mortuary attendants, they are happy enough with their lot. 'It's a nice line to walk,' one of them said, 'because you're stepping on wood. They've got the old pine sleepers on the Windermere – not like the mainline tracks which are laid on concrete and stones; they make your muscles ache and rip your boots to pieces. The original plate-layers' cabins, or what's left of them, are still here so, in wet weather, you can sit under a roof of beautiful Welsh slate to eat your sandwiches. Also, there are some good conifers growing along the way. They're fine trees and, when the Fisons weedkiller train comes down here each year, spraying, we make damn sure it don't do them any kind of mischief.'

Now, from Mr Russell's driving cab, I saw the cabins and the conifers and, crossing a high embankment, found myself looking down on the tops of a stand of giant beeches; there were rooks' nests in the branches, and the leaves seemed as bright as bullion. At Staveley station Mr Russell pointed to the deserted platform opposite. 'Since they took up the second set of tracks there has just been empty ground beside that platform. A while ago I came through here and there was a chap standing on it. I asked him what he was doing and he told me he was waiting for a train. I said, "But there's no railway over that side." "Aye," he said, after a thoughtful silence. "I were wondering about that."'

Mr Russell laughed and took off through woods and water-meadows, observing the old semaphore signals – the homes and distants – sounding his horn as he approached the crossings, pausing at Burneside to pick up an earnest young fell walker carrying a rucksack and maps, exchanging a wave with T. W. Dixon who was standing alertly by his barriers, and then rocking on to Kendal. I went back and talked to the fell walker, a teacher from the Ruhr who seemed bemused by the great antiquity of the rolling stock. 'In Chermany such a train would be found, I sink, only in the museum,' he said. A black American sitting nearby grinned at us. He wore a sharp three-piece worsted suit and had a folded ten pound note tucked in the silk band of his hat. 'In the US, man, such a train would be recycled into Buick convertibles,' he said.

When we had scrambled up through the copse and come to a halt at Oxenholme I said goodbye to Edgar Russell and, back on the platform, met a small, beaming, exuberant man who introduced himself as Alec Mayor, deputy advertising manager of the *Westmorland Gazette*. 'I'm a dedicated and incurable railway nut,' he explained. 'In fact, I started life working in the Windermere ticket office. But then they found that I had a bit of sugar and, British Rail needing diabetics like a hole in the head, I had to resign and resort to subterfuge. I became a railman *unofficial*.' His unofficial record is impressive. He reckons he has travelled a quarter of a million miles on the footplate, usually working his passage. 'It's a matter of knowing the drivers. If they think you're all right, they'll let you come along and lend a hand. I've fired to Glasgow for these chaps, even fired all the way to London. And I'll tell you what I used to do in my younger days. I'd get up at 4.45, go to Kendal station, catch the 5.45

Windermere Mail that had come down overnight from Euston and ride with it to Windermere. Then, I would drive the engine – Jubilee, Royal Scot or Britannia Class; I could handle them all – on to the vacuum table and turn it, back it up to the right end of the train, fill the water tank and give the fire a bit of attention, cleaning it and setting it up for the next run. When I'd done with that train it became the 8.10 to Manchester and I would return on it to Kendal, pop home for a bath, get into a suit and rush off to work at the *Gazette*. I did that every day for blooming *years*, and I loved it.'

The parcels traffic shipped from Windermere included regular consignments of mass-produced coffins. 'They were made by Nicholson's, down at Bowness,' Mr Mayor recalled, 'and they were brought to the guard's van neatly stacked on platform barrows. I was on the footplate one day when a woman walked past and saw a pile parked beside the engine. She looked at them and turned such a funny colour I thought she were going to faint. "Don't worry, love," I called, "they're only some instruments belonging to the Hallé Orchestra." Next thing I heard she was in the booking office, pestering some poor clerk for a ticket to the concert. Aye, the Windermere may be of no consequence any more but, goodness me, in my time I've had more fun on this little line than a cageful of monkeys.'

East Lancs' stubborn survivor

PRESTON TO COLNE

The hourly Preston to Colne service is operated by a pair of venerable coupled DMUs – Diesel Multiple Units – painted, appropriately, in British Rail's woad-like blue. There is a driver's cab at either end and it carries a guard who, because most of the stations at which it calls are unmanned, must also sell tickets. The line runs east, out towards the Pennines and through seventeen towns. Half a million people live along its twenty-eight-mile length; since many are too poor to afford a car, their dependence on the train is considerable.

This is the stretch of Lancashire which invented the spinning machine, built up a mighty industry and was then brought to its knees by Third World workers obliged to man their looms for loose change; today the train goes past empty, ornate mills as big as palaces, fine churches, majestic town halls built to celebrate forgotten civic splendours. 'Grand town halls,' a railwayman said to me. 'Aye, it's what the East Lancs line is known for.'

The Colne service departs from platform two at Preston's echoing glass and iron station; passengers must cross a bridge which segregates them from the profitable platforms accommodating the sleek Inter-City monsters. They board their funny little twin-carriage train and, usually bang on time, the old diesel rumbles and strains and, with a plume of smoke pouring from the roof, moves slowly away down a six-track section as broad as a motorway and spangled with coloured lights.

On a recent journey, having found a seat at the front, I struck up a conversation with the driver, Mr Des Harrison. A sturdy, reflective, quietly spoken man who has spent forty-three years with the railways, most of them on the footplate, he apologised wryly for the state of the rolling stock. 'It's shot at, absolutely *shot* at,' he said, turning right off the main thoroughfare as the automatic signal bells jangled in his cab. He drew my attention to them. 'Today's signalling is just beautiful. Before, if the fog was really thick, we had to hang buckets up on the old semaphores. When the signals came down the buckets fell off and you knew, from the clanking, that you were clear to go. But they could injure folk passing below; one chap near Wigan took a bucket on his head and, for weeks afterwards, he couldn't see straight.'

The Lancashire and Yorkshire railways were a tough training ground for drivers. No other area had such a profusion of lines, so many signal boxes – an average of thirteen to every ten miles of track – or precipitous hills, tunnels, cross-overs and goods loops. Now we trundled through a landscape

Mr Des Harrison. A reflective man who has spent forty-three years on the railways.

23

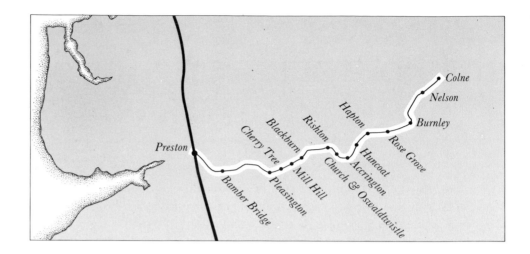

of electricity pylons and fields faded to the colour of kelp and, moments later, descended cautiously into Bamber Bridge, a station where the level-crossing sits smack at the end of the platform and remains menacingly open even when the train is in. Motorists passed within a few feet of Mr Harrison's cab, and those new to the area gazed up at him with their mouths open, visibly shaken. He said he knew how they felt. 'Many's the winter morning I've come here on a steamer, running on a bad rail, maybe greasy, maybe with ice or leaves on it, and I'd be coming down the hill with my whistle going and them gates open and my heart thumping like a drum.'

The crossing is manned. Its custodian sits in a lofty timbered cabin next to a tobacconist's shop and, when he had lowered his barriers, we headed for the tiny rural halt of Pleasington through rolling fields and green valleys dotted with farms. I saw a tumbling stream which might have held trout and a handsome village church with twin steeples. 'Some very nice homes around here,' said Mr Harrison. 'Posh area; plenty of money.' He pointed to an abandoned cutting leading away through the woods. 'The watermarked paper for printing Treasury bank notes on used to come along there.'

We rolled down an incline into Pleasington and halted between massed banks of autumnal oaks and beeches. I could hear birdsong even above the snuffling and grunting of the diesels. 'It's all unmanned now,' he said. 'But, until the Fifties, there would have been early and late turn porters here, early and late turn booking clerks *and* a station-master.' He peered down at the rails. 'They're wet,' he said. 'Dew. The sun hasn't got to them yet. It's all them trees.'

The gradient took us on to Cherry Tree and then, as abruptly as leaving a sunny garden for a cold, unlit room, we found ourselves entering Mill Hill and a bleak prospect of high-rise council flats, grimy houses, Thwaites pubs and, of course, mills; the names flickered by – Hawkins, Duxbury, Neale, Plantation and Wm Birtwistle – all the way to Blackburn where, sitting in the station, Mr Harrison said, 'My home depot, this. I started off as a call boy then graduated from traction trainee to driver's assistant, or fireman. You were expected to

ABOVE
The Bamber Bridge box at the turn of the century. It is still in use today.

LEFT
An indicator board, Blackburn station, 1964.

learn the roads by firing over them and when you became a relief driver, known in my day as a passed fireman, you got all the rubbish, all the late or dirty trips the drivers didn't want to make. After a three-day steam test you qualified as a proper driver, and often you started on night work. There were a lot of night traffic in them days: milk trains from Clitheroe, fish from Fleetwood – I recall the Fleetwood shrimp women travelling in their shawls and shrimping hats – coal from all over, quite a bit of fruit and such. Banana boats used to come up the Ribble direct from Jamaica to unload at Preston dock. Fyffes. Aye, I've carried a Jamaican banana or two down this line in my time, I can tell you.'

The train leaves Blackburn through a three-hundred-yard tunnel, passes a derelict mill, rattles on to Rishton, then plunges down across the Aspen Valley to Church and Oswaldtwistle, an ascending battlement of slate roofs with the gleam of water everywhere: the Leeds and Liverpool Canal snakes around the gaunt flank of a hill below, there are compensating reservoirs and, down on the valley floor, a stream frothing with the soft Pennine water that is so good for cotton.

Accrington comes next, an amphitheatre of smoke-blackened stone punctuated by tall chimneys. Gilbraith, Broughton's and Crown Mills, said the signs, but what Accrington was really celebrated for (apart from the beautiful hammered silver chalice in its church) was its eight-road depot and its shed – the head shed of the whole East Lancs system. Also for its notorious triangular platform and the yawning space that opened up, at certain points, between it and the carriages; arriving passengers were obliged to take their courage in both hands and perform terrific standing leaps just to leave the train. They had the Klondyke shunting engines here, together with the little Egberts and the famous Wigan Pigs; one of the local Pig drivers always carried a pot of mutton fat on the footplate for greasing his big end bearings. 'They were right buggers, some of them early drivers,' Mr Harrison remarked, surveying the empty grassy yards that had once contained all this activity. 'Very autocratic. Except to ask your number they wouldn't speak hardly one word from beginning of shift to end.'

A uniformed porter hopped aboard with a broom and, as we pulled out, he said he was off down the line to sweep the unmanned Huncoat and Hapton platforms. The former nestled in the fold of a valley, the latter commanded fine views of the worn country beyond, now dark and bruised by cloud shadows. There were rusty tracks and antique buffers here, too, but nothing to compare with those at Rose Grove, our next halt, where they once had a shed stabling fifty steam engines and accommodation for over a thousand wagons. This was where the Paddiham loop – a diversion starting at Blackburn and full of alpine gradients – came out, accommodating the wheezing trains carrying coal for Buckingham Palace; until management decided to use tarpaulins, an awful lot was pinched, the sport of swiping the King's prime quality nuggets being almost as popular as soccer. They ran Togo tank engines at Rose Grove, and the nippy little Rail Motor Locos with their lobster-pot spark arresters, and you could always identify a Rose Grove steamer because there were shoals of

The Accrington viaduct soon after completion.

BELOW
The twenty-one men who staffed Accrington station late last century. Today their work is done by a staff of four.

A lone signal box seems to be monitoring road traffic as well.

26

ACCRINGTON.

must not cross
the line

*Rose Grove in 1967, when there was
accommodation for fifty steam engines
and over a thousand wagons. Today the
place is abandoned, sad and charmless.*

minnows in its tender. The water was taken aboard from the Leeds and
Liverpool Canal, and generations of these extensively travelled little fish lived
out their lives being hurried blindly about the country in their small, jolting,
sunless worlds.

Today Rose Grove is a sad and charmless town. There is no fragrance in the
air, only the sour smell of deprivation. It was a relief to move off to Burnley
Barracks, once a Lancashire Regiment boot camp and then, down in the valley
where the Calder and Brun meet, to Burnley Central itself. 'Great place for
parcels, Burnley,' Mr Harrison said as we pulled in and, while they paused to
load a few, I wandered back through the train. Two men in donkey jackets were
lounging in the smoker. One said he hadn't worked for two years and, given the
gormless way his Job Centre was carrying on, he probably never would again.
The other had a position at a local cotton mill, but it was about to close; chances
were, he wouldn't ever be suited either. I moved on and chatted to a lady going
to visit a friend in Colne. She was small and neat, with shrewd eyes, and she told

me that she and her husband ran a theatrical costumier's business in Manchester. 'We do complete costumes with accessories,' she said. 'If you came in, chap your size, and with the stock we got at the moment, we could fix you up as a Rabbit, an Executioner, a Druid, a Squaw or a Bat.'

I moved on, then remembered that someone had given me a page photocopied from a Burnley literary journal containing a couple of contemporary tributes in verse to Jim Redford, a local engine driver who had died in 1887. Dropping into a vacant seat, I noted that '"Old Jim" – The Engineer' (Tune – Old Towler) contained lines like 'That good old man we all admire,/They call him railways Jim;/He bids the stoker mind the brake,/Then with his whistle clear/He makes the sleepy pointsman quake,/Old Jim the engineer!' 'Old Jim, The Engine-Driver' (Tune – Poor Mary Ann), on the other hand, was a notably gloomy affair, full of railway symbolism and metaphors. 'Now, alas,' it said, 'old Death has shunted/Dear old Jim!/Now his final trip is ended,/Poor old Jim!' But old Jim was clearly destined to enjoy a trouble-free run up to the Great Drivers' Mess in the Sky. 'Angel trains express are speeding,/Heavenward pointing signals reading,/Danger lamps are fast receding,/Glorious Jim!'

I put the paper back in my pocket. An elderly man with sunken eyes and a prominent, bony nose clambered aboard, carrying a shopping bag. The ancient, metal-fatigued door refused to close behind him so I went to help, attempting to slam it. But it repeatedly bounced back so, to get a better purchase, I jumped down and tried from outside. The guard, heavy and anxious looking, winced at the noise and seized the door in both hands. Making the small adjustments of someone manipulating a piece of wayward but familiar machinery, he closed it with a tiny click, sealing it snug as a bank vault. He smiled at me. 'Now we're all suited,' he said, and hurried off down the platform.

My friend, who had been watching in the doorway, lowered the window and said. 'You shouldn't have got out.'

'Why not?'

'Because now you have to get back in again.'

I considered the matter a moment. 'I could always use another door.'

'Aye.' He nodded slowly. 'Good thinking,' he said and, when I had joined him, offered me a toffee. Absently polishing his spectacles on the hem of his shabby coat, he said that he too was going to Colne. I told him that I was writing about the line and, as we moved away through a veined network of abandoned tracks, he said, 'In the old days Colne *was* railways. We had regular services to Manchester, Stockport, Wilmslow and Blackpool, and three trains a day right down to Euston. And they were good drivers, the Colne men – outstanding time-keepers, and well-known for it. They were busiest probably on Grand National Day; then you got steamers going out, one after the other, heading for the racecourse station near Fazakerley Junction, joining the engines working the horse box specials, bringing the steeplechasers in.' He unwrapped a Quality Street. 'We had Atlantics coming here. It were an

The line plunges from calm green fields into built-up industrial areas and back again.

The legendary Jim Redford.

Atlantic, working the 5.55 Boat Express out of Fleetwood, that went into a cattle train at Bamber Bridge and killed twenty pigs. Aye. We had the Baltic Quads here also, said to be unsteady riders, and the Agecroft Peacocks too. Did you know that King George V and Queen Mary came up this line to Colne in the summer of 1913? That were a Hughes Four Cylinder with polished buffers, Belpaire firebox, super-heated steam.'

I was trying to imagine the country so full of railways that it must have seemed, like a giant clock, to be nothing less than the sum of its moving parts, when we pulled into Brierfield, alongside the Smith and Nephew mill with red geraniums in its windows. 'I remember,' said my friend, 'when you couldn't move in the booking office here for cress. It was from the Duerden place and they used to stack so much in there it were like buying a ticket in some jungle clearing.'

The character of the line had begun to change. Semaphore signals were appearing outside and, as we approached Nelson, running past tree-lined streets and comfortable houses set in trim gardens, I went back to see Mr Harrison. 'These Nelson folk are very railway-minded,' he said, coming to a halt. 'We always get the biggest load of passengers at Nelson, and they're mad keen here on the special weekend excursions – them Merrymaker Mystery Trips, Rail Ramblers and so forth. But what is interesting now is that we've passed outside the Preston power signalling system. The box at Chaffers Sidings is looking after us and that's manual, the old semaphores. Also, a funny thing is about to happen to this line.'

What happened was that the dual track suddenly melted away beneath our wheels and became a single way. At the Chaffers Sidings box, set in a grove of trees, the signalman leant out and handed Mr Harrison a stout staff cut from oak. 'While I have possession,' he said, 'the line is exclusively mine and, if I forget to pick the staff up, I am faced with instant dismissal. This is a staff line, this is, single-track, and you wouldn't want another chap sharing it with you, particularly if he were proceeding in the other direction. On the way back I slow at the box and hand it in again.' He gestured over the trees, 'Victory V Gums. You heard of them? Very famous sweets. Over there is where they make them.'

Our approach to Colne was leisurely, the train suddenly floating out across a lofty viaduct, the town stolidly ascending the hill to the right, the majestic premises of John Pilling and Sons, Loom Makers, est. 1819 – now hung with To Let signs – way below us on the left. The station, a single small platform with a vandalised bus shelter standing on it, was set in a field of long grass. The land which had once held the sheds and tracks remained as flat as a bowling green. Beyond lay the weathered redbrick bridge, set in trees and wide enough to take three trains together, through which the expresses had once sped off up to Yorkshire. 'Bonny Colne on the Hill,' said Mr Harrison, picking up his oak staff and driving handle and making his way to the other end of the train. 'That's what they call it.' There was an eight-minute turn-around and Mr Harrison, relaxing in his cab, recalled some of the men who had worked the line before him. 'There were G. H. Lancaster, a real eccentric, and Wilf Marriot, who drove in spats and a bow tie. And Freddy Brown, a tiny chap, though, by God, he couldn't half go. *Drive?* I fired for him to Carlisle once and the carriages were rocking so much the passengers got seasick; at our destination they all staggered into the buffet for brandies.' Mr Harrison permitted himself a brief laugh. 'And there were another bloke, always wore clogs, who were a very unassuming railway fanatic. I used to fire for him too, and he had a little watch in his waistcoat pocket and he'd take it out, hours before we got to, say, Gannow Junction, and announce, "We will reach Gannow Junction, Des, at 10.32 precisely," and, by gum, we always did. To the *minute*. Brilliant, he were.'

To stave off the spectre of closure that has long dogged the line – built in 1846 by an engineer named Hattersley – a passengers' committee, including many of the irrepressible enthusiasts from Nelson, has planted flowers in the desolate, haunted ground around Colne station. 'I suppose we're doing this mostly to cheer ourselves up,' one of them admitted. 'Though on a more practical note we're also trying to get the line appointed official carrier of the garbage of the seventeen towns up to the Central Lancashire Incinerator. The authorities are blowing hot and cold on that one, but if they ever give us approval then the East Lancs could almost certainly pay its way.'

The half million people who live along its length are unlikely to surrender their trains without a fight. They are the descendants of the resourceful folk who deeply impressed Cromwell at Preston when, faced with an ammuniton shortage during the climactic battle which finally crushed the Stuarts, they ripped the lead from their church roof and melted it down into bullets. Burnley has produced two VCs, while Colne's most famous son, Wallace Hartley, was bandmaster of the *Titanic*. This was the man who coaxed a fine rendering of 'Nearer, My God, To Thee' (a few dissenting survivors said it was actually the episcopal hymn 'Autumn') from his musicians only moments before the certainty of a terrible death. When his body was brought home – by train – the procession which marched it up the hill from the station included the members of a symphony orchestra, a choir, a formation of bugler Scouts and the brass bands of Colne, Trowden, Nelson, Brierfield and Mount Zion. A hushed and reverent crowd of thirty thousand people lined the route. Hartley was buried in the evening dress in which they found him, drifting 380 miles off Cape Race clutching his violin case. Colne may not be the august railway capital it once was, but his presence there ensures that the old line still concludes its run with something of a flourish.

Wonder of the
Northern World

SETTLE TO CARLISLE

The late Dr Eric Treacey, Lord Bishop of Wakefield, maintained that the three chief wonders of northern England were York Minster, the Roman Wall and the Settle to Carlisle Railway. Dr Treacey, a lifelong train enthusiast – and a celebrated photographer of locomotives – was known up and down the metals as The Railway Bishop. His broad and varied church incorporated the whole national network and, though he had travelled all over it and knew every engine shed and rural railhead like the back of his hand, the Settle to Carlisle run seems to have maintained a special place in his affections. As a young parson he hitched rides on the footplates of its steamers, even borrowed a shovel and fired up the notorious Long Drag. He was one of the few men to have performed that exhausting feat for pleasure, and when he included the line among his list of illustrious landmarks, it was not out of sentiment, but from a precise knowledge of its monumental proportions.

The Settle to Carlisle, though only seventy-two miles long, is probably the greatest run in England. It is the *King Lear* of railroads, an epic route conceived in a fit of rage and driven recklessly across the kind of country that the SAS might choose for endurance training. Scores of men died during its construction. They perished from cold and disease, they fell off viaducts, were drowned in bogs and crushed by rockfalls; others simply gave in to despair and hanged themselves. One tiny churchyard, at Chapel le Dale beside the permanent way, contains the remains of two hundred navvies and their dependants. Even when the line was finished it continued to be as intractable as ever, and numerous steam engines, called upon to play one of the most demanding roles in the English railway repertoire, conked out on centre stage or, to be more precise, halfway up one of its alpine gradients.

Ironically, it need never have been built at all. It merely duplicated an existing stretch of track already running from Lancaster to Carlisle – now used by the Euston to Glasgow Inter-City expresses – and owned by the London and North-Western Company. An ambitious rival firm, the Midland, lacking any access to Scotland, tried to get its passengers over the Border by arranging to attach Midland carriages to London and North-Western trains, but the alliance between the two was brief. When irate Midland passengers complained of being coupled to very slow coal specials or abandoned, mischievously, in remote sidings, the Midland manager, James Allport, announced, furiously, that he would build his own damned line.

A laden train clambers out of a tunnel.

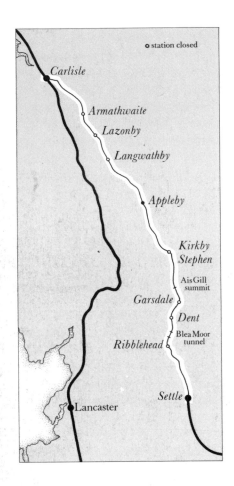

station closed

Carlisle
Armathwaite
Lazonby
Langwathby
Appleby
Kirkby
Stephen
Ais Gill
summit
Garsdale
Dent
Blea Moor
tunnel
Ribblehead
Settle
Lancaster

There was already a station at the town of Settle. With an imperious pencil stroke he joined it on the map to Carlisle and sent his application off to Parliament. Only then, accompanied by an engineer named John Crossley, did he trouble to cast an eye over the terrain. The two men walked much of the way and what they saw appalled them. This was a stretch of the high Pennines where the topography, conditions and weather conspired to produce perspectives from a nightmare. Cold and wet, they splashed across swamps, got lost, peered through the sleet at lofty hills and plummeting valleys and, nearing the top of their climb, grew deeply despondent when they reached 'that terrible place' Blea Moor. The average local rainfall was seventy inches, and much of it apparently contrived to come down that very day. But Allport and Crossley were messianic Victorian visionaries who, having voted God on to the Midland board years before, felt able to tackle the trickiest problems with equilibrium. They decided that what this wilderness needed, in effect, was some rather drastic landscape gardening and hurried home to start making arrangements. In 1866 the Settle to Carlisle Bill was approved by Parliament and at Appleby, the pretty little assize town midway along the proposed route, church bells were rung in celebration.

It took more than six thousand men six and a half years to lay that modest stretch of track which, once completed, promptly seized the public imagination and became the Blue Riband express route to the north. Travellers were stirred by its huge achievement and stunning scenery; it had a glamour and excitement which even infected Queen Victoria and her heirs; generations of Royal Pullmans have since swept along it to Balmoral.

Today, however, its only regular traffic is a bit of freight and the occasional passenger service between Leeds and Glasgow. After more than a century of hard usage, the line has been finally put out to grass, its metals worn down like the teeth of an old horse, its seventeen main viaducts getting a bit wonky about the legs. It has outlived its usefulness and, after closure, is likely to become yet another route destined to live on only in the ancestral memory of the kingdom's railway enthusiasts.

Recently I travelled down the Settle to Carlisle to keep an appointment in Appleby. The driver of the giant Class 47 diesel at Leeds station, seated in his spacious cabin, acknowledged my greeting with a lofty, ducal nod. But the carriages he towed were shoddy and forlorn and, as the train moved out, there was nothing about it to indicate that it was about to start a classic run. It takes fifty-seven minutes to get to Settle, cruising along the Aire valley into north Yorkshire, passing Ilkley Moor and trundling through Bell Busk to reach Hellifield where, high on a local crag, the Lancashire Witches lived; the station, standing at the head of the Settle to Carlisle, was once so posh that its staff included a French-trained cellarman.

At Settle Junction the line begins to climb; clattering across the points our diesel grew clamorous as it embarked on the Long Drag. During the next twenty-two miles we would ascend 740ft into the Pennines though, first, there was a brief stop at Settle where, to get it out of the wet, the line has been raised a

38

ABOVE
The Appleby box. The line on the left leads to Settle and Leeds, the one on the right to Warcop, where the church has a Norman nave.

LEFT
Settle station with leading porter Jim Baker. The structure is built from Bradford gritstone.

Dent Head viaduct.

foot or two. Jim Baker, the leading porter, waited with a set of wooden steps and offered them to a forlorn lady in black, who looked as though she had been away burying someone. The station, built from Bradford gritstone and neat as a new pin, is famous for its gardens, and I asked Mr Baker, a small, dapper man who wore his well-cut uniform with a swagger, where he got his flowers. 'Blackburn sends them up each spring,' he said. 'Boxes of annuals, mainly. French, Spanish and African marigolds; they'll flower here no matter what the weather. For the borders, Monica – she's the other leading porter – and me plant lobelias, with cotoneaster along the wall at back. It all makes a grand show in summer and, except for trimming them bloody privet bushes, I quite enjoy atttending to it.'

He glanced at his watch, stepped back and raised a hand. With a roar we were off, heading across the small viaduct passing the town. Settle nestles, prosperously and comfortably, in cave-riddled limestone hills opposite the Ribble valley and the venerable buildings of Giggleswick School, founded in 1512 and crowned by the lofty green dome of its chapel. 'I know a lad at Giggleswick,' a passenger remarked to me, 'and he tells me the school tolerates neither flogging nor fagging.'

Until recently, at this point in the journey, the guard walked through the train distributing glossy brochures entitled 'Highlights of the Settle Carlisle Line', but economies have put a stop to that, and few of the people around me appeared to know or care where they were. Noting my interest, however, the guard seemed happy enough to sit and talk. 'The navvies lived in shanty towns,' he said. 'There were, let's see, Jericho, Jerusalem, Sebastopol and Inkerman, Belgravia, Salt Lake City and Batty Green. They earned about 25p a day, and much of that went on booze. It were a rough life and it attracted rough types. There were so much drinking and brawling that the Midland started to worry about the men's immortal souls and sent missionaries to live and preach among them.'

Now a thousand feet up, we were approaching the celebrated Ribblehead viaduct, twenty-four arches across and over a hundred feet high. 'Bit of slack on the viaduct now,' said the guard, pointing to the thirty miles an hour speed limit sign. The crossing is dramatic enough to give one a momentary attack of vertigo. Way below was the frothing source of the River Greta and, somewhere, the remains of the kilns which fired the millions of superior bricks ('Tap them and they ring like pots,' their makers liked to boast) that now held us up in the sky.

'This place is very famous for its winds,' the guard remarked. 'They blow something ferocious. At north end they would have a team of men on gale duty, tightening the tarpaulins on the wagons before the crossing – but the tarpaulins were still frequently ripped off and would drift away across country like parachutes. I've even seen *cars* blown over the side. We had several wagons loaded with them one wild night a few years back; halfway over the viaduct, there were suddenly a terrific shower of sparks and, when we got to Dent box, the signalman shouted, "Lads! Three of thy Humber Snipes is missing!" And, by God, they were. We found them at first light, just scrap metal down in the stream bed below.'

The light was abruptly extinguished as, climbing hard, we entered Blea Moor tunnel, one and a half miles long and ventilated by three massive vertical shafts which, when the steamers went through – especially the double-headers – spewed volcanic clouds of smoke across the fells five hundred feet above. The tunnellers worked by candlelight and blasted with dynamite; one poor soul, unfamiliar with the properties of the stuff, died when he began drying a damp stick over an open fire. The tunnel starts in Yorkshire and ends in Cumbria and, out in the open again, we raced across two massive viaducts in quick succession, Dent Head and Arten Gill, the latter fashioned from a fossil-filled local sandstone known as Black Marble.

Then the line starts scoring points, dealing only in superlatives. Dent station, 1,150ft above sea level, is the highest station on any English main line (and it's closed). Garsdale station, at the far end of the 1,200yd Rise Hill tunnel, was, in the days of steam, famous for possessing the highest altitude water troughs in the world; it's closed too. Moments later, having progressed across the Dandy Mire viaduct, through the Moorcock tunnel, over Lund's viaduct and through

The Edinburgh to London express snowbound in the Dent cutting.

Ais Gill signal box, the highest mainline summit in England.

Shotlock Hill tunnel – Britain's highest – the wheezing engine brought us triumphantly to the Ais Gill signal-box, 1,169ft up, the top of the climb and the loftiest main-line summit in England.

The views around here are stupendous. The fells ripple leanly along the skyline, full of old muscle and sinew, some obscured by solitary showers swaying across them like dirty grey curtains, others gleaming in the wintry sun as though moulded from Roman glass. Down in the valleys there were streams, rivulets and small flash floods everywhere; further up, waterfalls gushed from the flanks of hills with the force of fire hydrants. We were descending fast now towards Appleby, the line navigating more tunnels and viaducts, carrying us through the huge shadow of Wild Boar Fell and past Kirkby Stephen, a township with an ancient butter market, a lovely red sandstone church and the ruins of a stately home where James I once came to dinner.

It was owned by the Wharton family; Philip Wharton had his portrait painted by Van Dyck and wrote the words of the song 'Lillibullero', now a signature tune of the BBC World Service; his birthplace is to be found between

Appleby from the station bridge. When the Settle to Carlisle Bill was approved by Parliament in 1866, church bells were rung in celebration here.

Birkett tunnel and Smardale viaduct. The next settlement along, Crosby Garret, has a tunnel named for it and, leaping the valley of Scandal Beck, a terrific viaduct too. It's an enchanting little place, tucked away below the railway, its venerable church containing a pair of bells; one, said to chime with particular sweetness, may have been cast in the thirteenth century.

Norman Greenhow was waiting for me on Appleby station – the only stop on the run. A tall, gruff, well-preserved man who keeps his own counsel, he worked on the Settle to Carlisle (with a few interim postings to other parts of the Carlisle District Promotion Area) from 1937 until the summer of 1981. Though retired, he still uses his old station-master's office and, sitting at a platform-sized desk, he said, 'I started here as a shunter working on locos such as Midland Compounds, Midland Fours and Crabbs; one of my jobs was to help get the London milk train ready for the evening run up to Express Dairy sidings at Cricklewood. My old man were the Crosby Garret village blacksmith and I'd have joined him but Mr Williams, the station-master, a grand chap, came and said he were looking for a porter. I took the job and never regretted it, though

Norman Greenhow supervised Appleby station until the summer of 1981.

things aren't the same now; there were greater companionship on the railway, war and pre-war, and more of us to share it. At Appleby today there are only two staff, two leading porters, but when I came there were . . .' He pondered a moment, frowning, then ticked them off on his fingers, 'station-master, chief clerk, two passenger clerks, goods clerk, two shunters, porter *and* goods porter. Nine men. Mind you, this were a very busy place. Plenty of stopping trains, plenty of freight. And everyone took water at Appleby. On the Up. Most did on the Down, too.'

He showed me around his little mock-Gothic brick station. The windows were mullioned, the pitchpine barge-boards intricately cut by a craftsman with a fondness for small stylistic flourishes, the ironstone platform verge kept as white as foam. Indoors, the waiting-room was freshly painted in grey and white, there were geraniums on the windowsills and, on the wall, a framed certificate stating that Appleby had been 'Highly Recommended in the 1979 Competition for Cleanliness and Tidiness'. The room contained chairs, a polished wooden table and an unlit coal stove, blackened till it shone. 'We'll get that going in a week or two, when the days start to draw in,' said Norman. 'It can get perishing here, though I'm not averse to winter myself. I like it when there's snow on the ground and a strong sun on your back.'

He conducted me into the ticket office. The floor gleamed and the brasswork glittered like newly minted sovereigns. 'That's Harold's doing,' said Norman. 'He polishes the brass, fills coal buckets, does all the odd things that need to be done.'

Harold has been coming to the station, daily, for thirty years, but he has no title and receives no salary. Indeed, he has no job; his work there is a labour of love and, in recognition of his efforts and seniority, he has been given, a few doors down from the parcels office, a snug little room of his own. He suffers from a speech impediment and communicates animatedly by sign and gesture; someone told me his father had been a railwayman and, when I asked what kind of work he had done, Harold pantomimed a man striding along the permanent way, peering at the track with unusual authority and attention. 'He were a superintendent on the line, Harold's old man,' said Norman, leading me away down the platform and along the rails to the signal-box.

There is a small junction by the box, a branch line heading away across the fields to Warcop, a village where the church has a Norman nave and, each year, celebrates Rushbearing Day. 'But it's mainly army there now,' said Norman, as we trudged through failing light and a fine rain. 'There's a big base up at Warcop, and the only traffic is explosives, ammo, boots and suchlike. The lads do a lot of their training at night; I often see them when I'm putting cat out.'

The signal-box is a lofty structure reached by a steep wooden stairway. A coal stove hissed and crackled cosily inside, the kettle was on the hob and the lamp lit. The signalman, wearing carpet slippers, sat in a battered armchair, reading. 'How's life treating you, Norman?' he asked, looking up and closing his book. Norman said he couldn't complain and, while they chatted, I examined the battery of ancient manual levers still being used to control the line. Each was clearly labelled: Up Main Detonator, Up Main Starting, Up Main Home, Run-round Siding To Up Main and, above them, I noted a worn Morse Code key. The rain, heavier now, beat on the windows, falling from lowering gunmetal clouds; in the west, though, up over Buttermere, the sky was clear, the colour of lemons. In the box I thought I could smell fresh toast.

I remarked to the signalman, a slim, alert, dark-haired young man, that he had got himself a very nice number indeed, and he grinned. His name was Paul Holden and he said that, for six years, he had been manager of a Berni Inn at Bristol. 'We lived in a flat above the premises with our small son and kept worrying about what kind of life we were offering him. Also, I was getting fed up with the rat race and, finally, there came a moment when I either had to commit myself to a career or get out. I'd always had a secret ambition to work on the Settle to Carlisle; I've been a train spotter since I was eight and I've travelled up and down the line as an enthusiast more times than I can remember. So I rang Carlisle on the off-chance that there might be a vacancy, and they offered me the Appleby signal-box!' His colleagues at Berni Inns thought he was off his trolley; details of his new salary merely confirmed this belief. 'But you can live cheaply here,' Paul said. 'We've bought a cottage, my son goes to the local school and loves it, we've got the perfect existence. And I've got my trains.' He pointed to a Pentax camera lying loaded and ready on the table. 'I photograph them all. I shoot them from the box, I come to work three hours early and shoot them around the station, I go out on moonlit nights and, using fast film and a wide aperture, shoot the traffic passing through. I shoot everything that moves on this line. That's the thing about the Settle to Carlisle: you get so involved with it. It isn't a job; it's a full-time preoccupation.'

The electric bell rang several times and Paul, jumping up, repeated the sequence on his Morse key. 'A Four One,' he said, pulling down a signal lever, 'and the bell code tells me it's a Fitted Freight. What you heard was Culgaith box offering me the train, which I have accepted and cleared through Appleby. Actually, he'll stop here for a moment to pick up the drinking water for the box on Blea Moor; it's sent up every evening. We usually pass the freights straight through but if, say, there's a high-speed Express Parcels close behind – that's bell code One Three One – I'll shove him in the siding here and give precedence to the Parcels.'

Norman pulled a shiny silver hunter from his waistcoat pocket. 'Reckon it were time we were off,' he said, putting it back. 'Hell of a good timekeeper, this watch,' he remarked, patting it, and we walked back to the platform as Paul's Four One freight, hauling a clanking procession of hoppers, halted briefly while the driver jumped down and grabbed a pair of plastic jerrycans marked 'Blea Moor Signal Box Drinking Water Only'. 'You get granite travelling on this line,' said Norman, 'and limestone and pig iron and Sardinian perlite for the British Gypsum place down at Newbiggin.'

We went to have some supper. 'The most outstanding thing about the Settle to Carlisle,' said Norman, drinking soup, 'is wind. Around here you get Helm Wind, which is local, and sometimes you can see it, a high black cloud sticking

The first snows of winter fall on the high fells.

At Garsdale the turntable was surrounded by a wall of sleepers to prevent the engines being spun by the wind.

straight up in the sky; it can be bloody draughty, Helm Wind, but nowt like what you get down at Ribblehead, where I've crossed the viaduct on my hands and knees. Sometimes steamers used to get critically short of power because wind kept blowing the coal off fireman's shovel. Or the train would be stopped dead in its tracks, held fast by the force of the gale. At Garsdale they had their turntable entirely surrounded by a shield of sleepers. It were put up due to an incident in 1900 when wind caught a loco that were being turned and spun the bugger like a top, whizzing it uncontrollably round and round for an hour or more.' He ordered some fish and continued, 'You get other hazards, too. In Rise Hill, one of the wet tunnels, there were recently a two-ton icicle dangling from a ventilation shaft. We had teams watching that icicle day and night; if it had got out of control a loco could have been damaged. The gangs always patrol the line for icicles, knocking them down with sticks, and they usually get to them before they become dangerous.' I asked whether they had suffered many accidents on the line. 'Aye,' said Norman, 'quite a few come to mind. Recently, for example, there were this off-comer, a football fan, who had a few sherbets too many and fell out of the Scotch Up. We only knew because one of our lads, a driver who had done the run the day previous and were coming home on the cushions, noticed a door were open. When you fall off these trains you cartwheel, and if you cartwheel in a tunnel, well, you can imagine what's left of you is fit for.'

'Yes, I can,' I said, hastily.

'*Haggis*,' said Norman. 'That's bloody what.'

50

Next morning I caught the train on to Carlisle. In the parcels office a pair of yawning baby eagle owls, bred at Appleby's graceful medieval castle, were awaiting transportation up the line to a private zoo. The castle was once the property of the celebrated Clifford family; George Clifford brought Elizabeth I the news of the Armada's defeat, and liked to wear her glove in his hatband. His daughter, Lady Anne, was a scholarly, single-minded woman who, when one of her tenants refused to pay his annual dues – a hen – took him to court, won the case and invited him home to dinner to share the hen with her.

The train, according to the Appleby clock (made by Potts and Sons of Leeds), was four minutes late and set off down the line at speed; the remainder of the trip, though, was a bit of an anti-climax. The final thirty-one miles to Carlisle still has its share of tunnels and viaducts, but the wild energy and demonic ambition of the first sector had given way to a more orthodox railway, the kind any self-respecting Victorian engineer could have laid with one hand tied behind his back.

What the route lacks in majesty, though, it makes up for in lovely Border landscapes and glimpses of the Pennines which, having veered sharply away, now shadow the line from a distance. Near Crowdundle viaduct the train crosses the Roman Road, at Little Salkeld it passes a Druid ruin called Long Meg and Her Daughters, close to Armathwaite it skirts a gorge, deep and wild as a Balkan ravine where, in season, the salmon run in from the Solway; on the very doorstep of Carlisle, at Scotby, it trundles past a house containing a pair of life-sized statues of Dutch haymakers, cast in lead and thought to have been the property of Nell Gwynn. Moments later it pulls up at Carlisle's Citadel station, an airy glass folly as graceful as a Ming pavilion.

But Appleby remains, in a sense, the keeper of the old line's conscience. This was demonstrated in May 1978, when Dr Eric Treacey, the Railway Bishop, died suddenly while photographing trains near the Down platform. Several months later a memorial service was held for him at the station. Three thousand people turned up, together with six bishops and three steam engines. After Mr D. S. Binnie, manager of the London Midland Region, had read from the First Epistle to the Corinthians ('Though I speak with the tongues of men and of angels, and have not charity, I am become as sounding brass, or a tinkling cymbal') there was a minute's hushed silence, begun and ended by the trumpet-like whistle of the Class Nine freight locomotive *Evening Star*, the last steam engine built in Britain.

The sea-washed line
by the Solway shore

CARLISLE TO BARROW

The line from Carlisle to Barrow-in-Furness follows an almost perfect curve around a hilly green shoulder of England. Once this particular territory was covered with railways, each delineating the fiefdoms of the tiny companies that had divided the fells up between them. They included the Cockermouth and Workington, the Furness, the Maryport and Carlisle, the Solway Junction, the Rowrah and Kelton Fell and the Lowca Light Railway, and they sent a tracery of lines spreading through Cumberland like veins on a leaf; all that remains today is that single set of tracks, running for 85¼ miles along the Irish Sea.

People were always railway-minded around here. They laid the world's first wrought-iron rails – for Lord Carlisle, who bought the Stephensons' original Rocket to run on them – and operated Britain's last horse-drawn train, the elegant little Port Carlisle Dandy Car, pulled by a single Clydesdale and able to accommodate twenty-seven passengers in three separate classes. The service was finally converted to steam in 1914.

The Barrow to Carlisle has the little idiosyncracies that go with age and a leisurely, somewhat eccentric evolution. When the Queen and Prince Philip visited one of its towns, Workington, they were unable to travel in the Royal Train because mainline stock cannot get around some of the bends or through two of the bridges. The service is operated by narrow twin-carriage diesels called Accrington Sets which are fitted with barred windows to stop the unwary poking their heads out. Some years ago a fireman leant from his footplate as he sped through a bridge and fetched himself the most terrible crack on the skull. Amazingly, it did not prove mortal and he is still to be seen around Carlisle. 'He gets about all right, though I doubt the poor chap would win "Mastermind",' a railwayman told me sadly.

The train pulls out of Carlisle's Citadel station and sets off on a south-westerly heading, trundling past the MFI Furniture Centre and through a weed-filled cutting. At this point it is no great distance from the site of the Solway viaduct, Europe's longest railway bridge and the city's own direct link with Scotland until ice floes rendered it unsafe; it was dismantled in 1934, after the Presbyterian authorities had complained that people were skipping church on Sundays and walking over to England to get a drink instead.

The first village on the line, Dalston, is approached through pastureland. It has a sleepy rural halt – unstaffed, request stop only – not far from the farmhouse where Susanna Blamire, the poetess known as the Muse of Cumber-

The line skirts a characteristic section of coast.

53

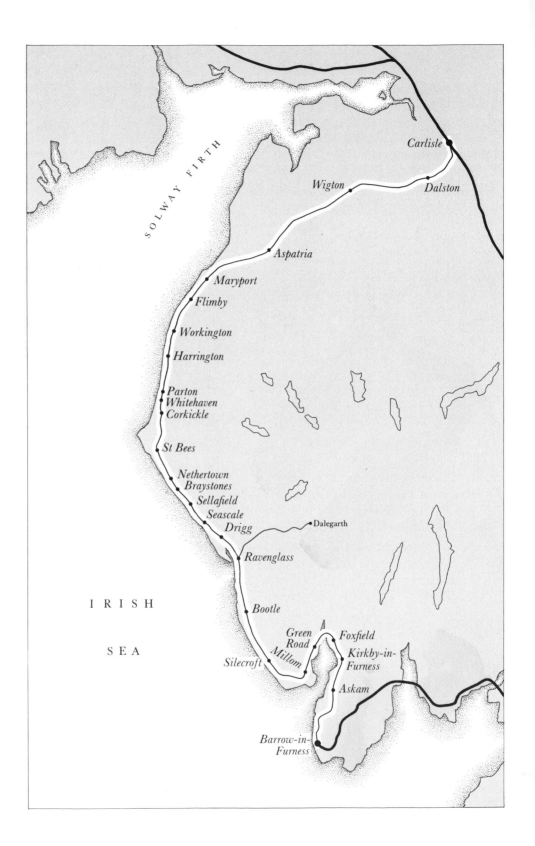

land, was born in 1747. At Wigton, next down the line, there is a large paper mill and at Aspatria, beyond the platform, the nondescript buildings of the Milk Marketing Board's Aspatria Creamery. This was once an important junction of the Maryport and Carlisle, a company founded to exploit the West Cumbrian coalfields. Though most of its trains – like the little Baggra Bus, which chugged in from Mealsgate (and Baggrow) – linked collieries, iron works and quarries, the line also served places like Wigton, famous for its jam factory, and Crofton, which had a private station. The company built most of its own locomotives, and it was at its Maryport workshops that George Tosh fitted an engine with the world's first steel boilers.

Maryport was founded to exploit the coal boom, too, but is chiefly remarkable for the discovery, last century, of twenty splendid Roman altars in pits close to the town. This coast was once thronged with Romans and their artefacts were two a penny, but the size of the find caused an expectant stir at the Maryport and Carlisle head office, located under a handsome clock tower on Maryport station; museums all over the country were clamouring for the altars and the Director of Freight didn't stop smiling for a week.

As we headed for Flimby and Workington I chatted to the guard, a young man named Raymond Cottier, who told me that it was a good run, this, plenty of variety, nice scenery, not much trouble. You got the odd traveller who was liverish or drunk, of course, but there was a strong community feeling along the line and other passengers invariably came to your assistance. 'There are a couple of big deaf-and-dumb lads who get on at Millom,' said Mr Cottier, 'and I can always depend on them to help me with troublemakers; I've seen those two pick up some miner looking for a fight and shove him back in his seat so hard it made his eyes water.' He suddenly gestured out the window. 'The sea!' he said, and there it was, looking sullen and cheerless in the thin, sharp November light, the steep little waves tripping over their own shadows and breaking in welters of foam which the wind snatched up and spat at the train. Scotland loomed across the Solway Firth like a bulky blue island, its hills cloud-dappled, and I looked straight along the route which Mary Queen of Scots had taken when she fled across the Solway in an open boat, landing at Workington and staying with the Curwen family; it was from their house that she wrote her celebrated letter to Elizabeth I, seeking forgiveness and a reconciliation.

Modern Workington is a city built by ironmasters and founded on coal and steel; in Workington Henry Bessemer dreamt up the process that was to revolutionise steel-making, and its approaches are grimy and unlovely. The yellow-brick station, however, was as smart as paint, its platform gardens raked and weeded, and, breaking my journey, I went to a large office by the Down platform to talk to David Langton, the traffic manager. Brisk, dark-haired and business-like, he told me that his station still had some of the old bullhead rails running through it; also, a few of the sleepers were made of iron, unique in Britain but a distinction Workington shares with Zaire and the Ivory Coast. The office contained a sizeable desk and, pinned to the wall, a copy of the

Guard Raymond Cottier. 'A strong community feeling along the line.'

The grimy approaches to Workington, a city built by ironmasters.

Sellafield with holiday caravans.

Whitehaven Tide Table. Mr Langton said, 'We have to keep an eye on that; at Cunning Point you can get the sea washing right up over the line.'

He called for coffee. 'The important thing about this line is that it's making money. We haven't got the volume of traffic we had pre-war,' he told me, 'but what we do have is regular and profitable: 4,500 tons of coal daily to Fiddler's Ferry power station near Warrington, regular shipments of ingot moulds down to Workington docks, shipments of pig iron and perlite coming out again. We carry high explosives to the Ministry of Defence weapons testing establishment at Eskmeals and, ten or twelve times a week, we operate the Specials that carry plutonium rods in and out of Sellafield, the nuclear power plant that represents the marriage of Windscale and Calder Hall.'

The man who keeps an eye on these volatile cargoes is Ron Copeland, the Area Movements Inspector. 'There are special rules for the carriage of gunpowder and high explosives; they're covered by the United Nations Code and, if anything goes wrong, the driver hops off his train, finds a phone and makes his coded call. If he can't locate a phone and is late passing a box then the signalman will realise that something is amiss and make the call instead. But even more stringent rules apply to nuclear fuels, and Crewe must give clearance before a wheel turns.

'Sellafield is the only British plant capable of treating the spent fuel rods from our other plants – all rail-connected, but for two – so there is constant traffic up and down this line. Add to that the nuclear waste that's shipped to Barrow from Italy and Japan and which also comes down the line for reprocessing, and you'll realise that British Nuclear Fuels are one of our biggest clients. It's a very good thing for employment in the area that they *are* here. In my dad's day we had agriculture, iron ore and hundreds of pits. Now the Haig colliery near Whitehaven is the only one left.'

The fuel rods, about a metre long, travel in fifty-five-ton reinforced flasks, one to a wagon. The drivers work their Plutonium Specials around the country just as they would an evening Parcels or morning Milk. One of them, Spencer Bromley, popped in for a moment. Mr Bromley, a personable man who looks a bit like Stanley Holloway, was once mayor of Workington; it was he who assured Prince Philip, still fretting slightly at a Town Hall reception, that the line could not possibly have accommodated the Royal Train. I asked him about the controversial freight that he and the other Workington drivers were obliged to carry, and he said, 'Oh, we just treat it as normal. We don't get the choice of an alternative load, and I can only remember one case of a man making trouble. That was a driver who said he was a conscientious objector and a member of the Greenpeace Organisation, though I don't recall what happened. I expect they just sent him off to Barrow docks to pick up a load of saucepans instead.'

I boarded another train and continued my journey south, past Harrington, an old coal port which possesses a church with a fine hammerbeam roof, then on through Parton to Whitehaven, Cumberland's third town. Whitehaven was the last place in Britain to suffer a foreign invasion when, in 1788, Paul Jones sailed in from America and tried to sack the place. But Whitehaven does nothing by halves. They fought him off with the same single-mindedness they had displayed during the last sixty years of the seventeenth century; then, realising they were sitting on huge deposits of coal, they enlarged their community from nine cottages to a busy settlement of over two thousand people. Today the shore deposits have all been worked out but, undeterred, the Haig colliery miners have burrowed under the ocean floor and are now working seams so far out to sea that one of them remarked, 'We'll soon be drilling through the water mains of County Down.'

The train pushed on past Corkickle, where comfortable houses on a grassy rise were confronted by fleets of ICI caustic soda wagons parked in the sidings. We rattled along the floor of a dark valley, and suddenly burst out into rolling farmland gilded with late afternoon sun. 'We're coming up to St Bees,' said Robert Armstrong, the guard. 'Very famous public school; they got real

J.F. Burrell del.ᵗ

A stretch of track in Victorian times.

upper-class kids there.' It was founded by Edmund Grindal, Archbishop of Canterbury, in 1583, and its mellow sandstone buildings are set in four hundred acres of the Valley of St Bees. The school – motto 'Expecta Dominium' – is now co-educational, and the only St Beghians I saw were two plump girl joggers in shorts who stood impatiently at the level crossing as we passed, their legs and cheeks as pink as strawberries in the frosty air.

The line returned us to the beach. There were holiday cottages on the foreshore, but they were shuttered and empty, glum little habitations as lifeless as caves and complemented by a colony of shoddy, deserted caravans on the

wrong side of the tracks. Then, up on the skyline, a remarkable apparition swam into view. Sellafield looks, from the line, like a futuristic city state crowned by silver domes and streaming silver chimneys. But though Britain's most venerable nuclear power establishment has become such a familiar component of the landscape that nobody on the train spared it a second glance – and nor did the scores of golfers playing unconcernedly on a course built right alongside it – its presence has clearly led to the creation of a few enduring Gothic myths. As we slid through Drigg and past a marsh famous for its wild geese, Mr Armstrong nodded at a distant grove of pines. 'They dump

An Edwardian steam train drops passengers at St Bees.

contaminated nuclear waste behind them trees,' he said. I chose not to believe him, despite the brisk affirmative nod of a nearby passenger who had overheard and, nearing Ravenglass, wondered what it must be like growing up in a place where, presumably, certain woods and copses were ruled out of bounds on the grounds that playing in them could turn you into a tadpole.

Ravenglass, the most ancient port in Cumbria, stands on the estuary where the Irt, Mite and Esk join the sea. This was also a famous Roman settlement; Caesar's fleets anchored off Drigg Point, forts were erected and roads built out across the fells. There are remains here, but what most people come to see is the celebrated narrow-gauge railway that runs up through Eskdale to Dalegarth. The tiny engines of the Ravenglass and Eskdale used to haul granite and terminate at Boot. Now they chug through the fells carrying enthusiasts, their drivers among the first in Britain to be equipped with two-way radios.

The miniature line ends beside a tea-room and a lovely old engine shed fashioned from pink sandstone. Above, the dark flanks of the Old Man of Coniston merged with a lowering sky so that, heading off towards Bootle, we seemed to be moving inside a dome of smoked glass. We passed a branch line leading to a white gate and a tall pole from which a red flag flew; there was a screen of trees and, behind it, a mysterious perspective of towers and cupolas. 'That's the Vickers' firing range,' said Mr Armstrong. 'Come past here sometimes and there's such a racket you can hardly talk to your passengers. They're shooting fit to bust, straight out to sea, like they was trying to sink Ireland.'

We had arrived at that stretch of coast, stretching from Carl Crag down to

Selker Bay, which is administered by the Ministry of Defence and given over to testing Britain's newest weapons. The sea along the battered foreshore looked bruised; small, lumpy waves smacked sullenly on the beach, the surf as discoloured as if kids had been washing their paint-brushes in it. Behind us, though, was the majestic edifice of Black Combe, a 1,970ft peak from which – on a clear day – you can see fourteen English and Scottish counties, together with the Isle of Man, Snowdon, the Irish coast *and* the Mountains of Mourne. At Silecroft, next station up the line, there is a penitentiary. 'Haverick open air prison,' said Mr Armstrong. 'And nearby, to keep the old lags happy, is a well-known nudist camp.'

He went off to sell tickets as we pulled away and headed for Millom, which has the choicest Station Hotel on the line, tree-shaded and chocolate brown, its windows picked out in white. In the church are the tombs of the Huddleston family; it was John Huddleston who administered the Last Sacrament to Charles II. We crossed Millom Marsh, saw the sweep of Duddon Sands and motored on past Green Road, a tiny halt flanked by empty fields; huge puddles glittered in the station yard and, at the level crossing, an audible warning device sounded with a curiously mournful note. The line, in sombre mood, passed Foxfield and skirted Angerton Marsh. At Kirkby-in-Furness a stern message painted on the front of a house warned that salvation could only be won through belief in the Lord. The war dead of Askam are commemorated by a memorial set hard by the station.

A giant diesel loomed up and growled past, towing empty wagons, its headlamps flaring in the dusk. Cold, dense rain was falling on Barrow, the city's shadowy outlines and sodium lights slipping metronomically in and out of focus as the windscreen wiper slapped back and forth. While still out in the marshes we had seen the dockyard cranes ranged along the evening skyline like a row of giant birds. Several, I knew, stood by the slipways where the Royal Navy's Polaris submarines were built, adding a further footnote to this strange, secretive line. Did the bubbling radioactive broth that fuelled the giant boats come down these metals? Together with warheads so accurate that they could *in theory* – or so a bespectacled man sitting across the aisle assured me – take out town hall clocks all over Russia? But then, abruptly, the track led us away from the waterfront and took us instead through a wilderness of derelict red-brick houses.

We were now moving through the heartland of the old Furness Railway, and were not far from the spot where, in one of the strangest incidents in British railway history, an engine was swallowed up by the ground. One October morning in 1881 Driver Postlethwaite and his fireman were doing a bit of shunting work when, all at once, the earth began to give way beneath them. They jumped for their lives and stood watching incredulously as their locomotive settled lower and lower and then, like a stricken ship, threw up its stern and vanished altogether. The engine, a Sharp D1 Class with Ramsbottom safety valves and a large oblong rear splasher, fell two hundred feet into an old mine where it remains – buried treasure of a kind – to this day.

High road to the Isles

GLASGOW TO MALLAIG

The ancient bull-nosed locomotive which takes the first train of the day down the West Highland line to the herring port of Mallaig readies itself for departure a few minutes before six. The early morning somnolence of Glasgow's Queen Street station is broken by the old diesel's deep, full-throated song, while blue smoke rings eddy up into the shadowy glass roof and those passengers not familiar with the rolling-stock give an involuntary start as they hurry towards it along platform five. The entire train, they suddenly note, is wreathed in steam. It hisses and swirls about the engine and four antique carriages, making them seem ghostly and insubstantial. Small wisps float around the station like random fragments of mist; aboard, steam drifts through the corridors as well, mixing with the musty, Edwardian-parlour smells of the panelled compartments.

The Highland lines are among the last in Britain to offer the homely comforts of the Mark One Non-Commonwealth Bogie Steam-heated carriages and though the guard, a modern-minded young man who hummed Strangler tunes and wore a fancy digital watch, was clearly embarrassed by the archaic arrangements, they seemed entirely appropriate to the 164¾-mile journey we were about to undertake, a trek along a winding single track through some of the most desolately beautiful country in Europe.

With the diesels straining thunderously, we moved off into a raw winter's morning, the driver taking a run at the notorious Cowlairs incline – up which, once, trains had to be winched by cable – and then bucketing through the dark while the rain slopped down the windows and a sea wind keened across the carriage roofs. I sat sleepily in a pool of lamplight, seeing my whey-faced reflection in the streaming black glass and, in other lit windows along the way, yawning people pulling on clothes, slumped at breakfast tables, perhaps glancing up blankly as we rattled by.

At Craigendoran we swung away from the Glasgow North electric lines carrying early commuter traffic and crossed on to the West Highland proper. Greenock was a pale smudge over the Clyde, glimpsed briefly before we headed up the deep, trench-like estuary of Loch Long towards the sweet water of Loch Lomond. At this time of the year, hereabouts, early morning visibility is similar to the kind you get through an infra-red gunsight, and Loch Lomond at 7am was just a prospect of shadows with Arrochar and Tarbet station a small oasis of platform lights in the gloom. A match flared near the parcels office and a

A rural station early one snowy morning on the road to the isles.

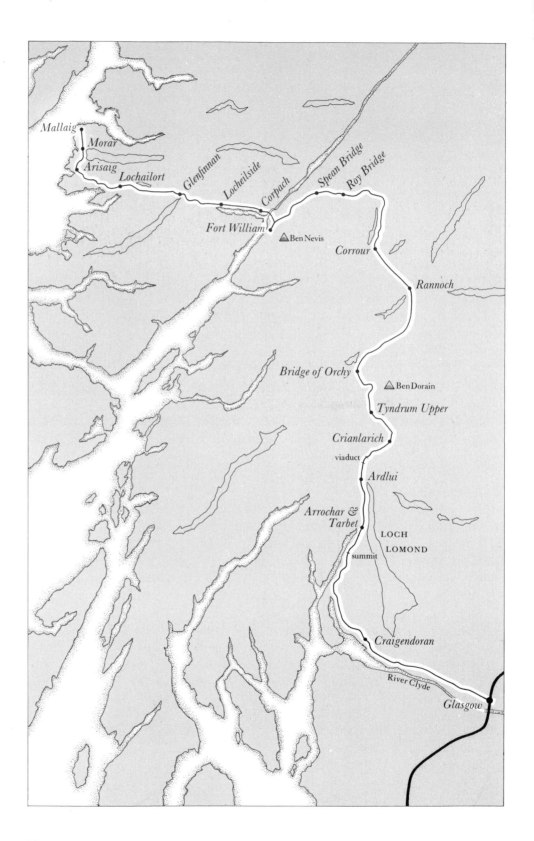

CUTTING THE FIRST SOD WEST HIGHLAND RAILWAY

Birth of the West Highland. Lord Abinger cuts the first sod.

smoker heralded the new day with a terrible seal-like bark which, mercifully, faded quickly behind us as we moved on to Ardlui.

The line had now descended almost to the water's edge. There was a tiny signal-box on the platform, softly lit and full of gleaming levers and, beyond it, the soft, stony splash of small waves falling on a shingle beach; as we headed up Glen Falloch at the start of a hard fifteen-mile climb, this water music grew and grew until it filled the train. We seemed to be running through the aftermath of a monsoon. Scores of burns were frothing down the hillside; the River Falloch, far below, was exuberantly in spate while the falls of Ben Glas tumbled 120ft to vaporise in a swirling fog and Inverarnan Water slid roaring beneath the line. The air was pearly and peat-smelling and damp enough to make the plumage of an escorting falcon gleam like oiled teak. Crossing the viaduct over the Dubh Eas Water the guard told me we were the same height above it as the Forth Bridge was above the sea. We stood together, gazing down, and I asked him whether he enjoyed working the route. 'Aye,' he said, 'it's a bonny run, though I'll like it even better when they give me one of the wee automatic ticket machines they've promised us.'

67

Crianlarich is the station at which the West Highland splits, one arm turning off to Oban, the other heading north through Strath Fillan at the start of its great meandering safari out to the Isles. Crianlarich has a lovely chapel-like engine shed fashioned from dressed stone, and refreshment rooms once celebrated for the excellence of their luncheon baskets; for twenty miles on either side the line used to be littered with champagne corks and the discarded shells of plovers' eggs. As we stood there, two notable things happened: the platform lights were switched off and several bulky packages were brought to the guard's van on a creaking blue barrow – bundles of the *Weekly News* and *People's Journal* destined for Mr Munro of Morar, R. K. McLean of the Harbour Shop, Mallaig, and Miss M. Mackinnon at the Post Office, Isle of Eigg. They were stacked beside a cello in a shiny white case, destined for Mr Wattie on Skye and taken aboard in Glasgow.

Outside the station the line crosses a viaduct and begins the climb to Tyndrum Upper, where the platform was planted with small flower-beds and spread with gravel, which crunched underfoot. A wind sprang up, rocking the train, making it creak like an old ship. The wind was still blowing as we approached the unique horseshoe curve which has become one of the most celebrated stretches of railway in Scotland. While edging cautiously around the rocky flanks of Ben Odhar the train suddenly comes face to face with Ben Dòrain, an elegant mountain so similar in profile to Fuji that the few Japanese who travel the line hiss with excitement when they see it. The track crosses a pair of aqueducts, then – precariously established on the steep sides of Dòrain – doubles back on itself, enabling the passenger to look across the abyss and note, imperceptible as a pencil stroke, the stretch of line he had been travelling a few minutes earlier.

The cloud base was sinking fast and, within minutes, we were inside it, bumping and swaying blindly along towards Bridge of Orchy and the spot where, many years ago, the celebrated runaway guard's van finally came to rest. It had become detached from the 2.15am Down express freight and, with its occupant sleeping peacefully in a chair beside his coal fire, had hurtled down the gradients and through the intervening stations, the signalmen at each frantically sounding their bells and offering the rogue van to the next box along. After an epic twenty-five mile dash it finally coasted to a halt at Bridge of Orchy, beaten by an upward slope as severe as a ski jump. The guard, a smile on his face, was still zonked out when they reached him. 'The way that wee bugger could sleep,' our own guard told us with pride, 'was *legend*.'

The line stalks the River Orchy all the way to its source at Loch Tulla and then passes the ruins of Achallader Castle, the ancestral stronghold of the Fletchers; Crannach Wood is one of the few remaining vestiges of the Great Caledonian Forest, burnt down to flush out the wolves and bandits. We were now drawing close to Rannoch Moor where, even in high summer, people die from exposure or drown in bogs and swamps. In winter the snow accumulates in drifts as high as sand dunes, and a certain stretch of railway track out on the moor is the only one in Britain equipped with a snow shed, or roofed stockade,

Crossing Rannoch Moor.

to protect it from the elements. But the train still gets stuck periodically, and an emergency hamper must be carried at all times. I asked the guard what it contained. 'Och, just Mars bars and such,' he said, adding that it was kept in his van, together with a ladder, an assortment of axes and the ambulance box. Among the items stored in the box, according to a notice, were '1 First Aid Leaflet Form 1008 (1958), 24 Sterilised Finger Dressings, 12 Waterproof Adhesive Wound Dressings, 1 Tube of Eye Ointment, 8 Eye Pads, 12 Safety Pins (Rustless), 1 List of Contents and 1 Label (BR 7171/15) Pasted to Outside of Box'.

The train starts out across Rannoch Moor at Gorton Crossing, where the wilderness probably looks much as it did when Robert Louis Stevenson wrote about it in *Kidnapped*: 'The mist rose and died away and showed us that country lying as waste as the sea; only the moorfowl and the peewits crying over it and far over to the east a herd of deer moving like dots . . . A wearier looking desert man never saw.' The moor was a camouflage patchwork of browns and greens with tiny ribbon lochs, tarns, ditches and aimless meanders scattered through

69

the peat hags; when the sun broke through for an instant the whole landscape suddenly rippled with light, the brief glitter reminding me that it was possible, in winter, to skate from one end of the moor to the other and, in summer, to cross it with a non-stop swim. Both feats have been achieved.

Moments later an odd thing happened. Without any warning the train began to bounce. The action was gentle but persistent and, as we went hopping on our way, the buffet car attendant explained that it was due to the depth of the bog. 'They couldn't find the bottom to lay proper foundations on,' he said, 'so the track was floated along a raft of larch saplings set on a mattress of earth and ash. The trouble is, the whole section starts doing this crazy little dance whenever a train crosses over it.'

A steam train occupies a siding at Tulloch station.

773

N.B.R. Tulloch Station from Bridge.

A light powdering of snow lay around Rannoch. The chalet-style station building, set on island platforms, is painted in the two contrasting shades of green which have always been a hallmark of the West Highland; the birch shingles on the walls, another hallmark, were brought from Switzerland. The train pulled in with a sigh, blowing steam all over the place. I disembarked and found Donald McLellan, the station-master, in the post room, sorting mail for distribution to Rannoch School, Easter and Wester Carrie, Dunan Manse, Bridge of Ericht and Crosscraig Lodge. It would be delivered in the orange Mercedes van I could see standing beside Rannoch's lone telephone box.

Mr McLellan, the job finished, led me down the platform to his office. A coal fire crackled and smoked in the grate and the ornate longcase clock ticked thunderously. 'It only misses a beat a day,' he remarked. Pinned to it was a typewritten list saying 'Fog and Snowstorm Roster' and nearby stood one of the famous West Highland interstation telephones, which were built with such extraordinary powers of amplification that the voice coming out of the receiver could be clearly heard fifteen feet away. There was also a bright red token machine, electrically activated by the next signalman up the line. Since the West Highland is a single-track railway, no driver may set off along it until the machine has released his heavy, key-shaped steel token, or pass. 'If the machine fails,' said Mr McLellan, 'we must send the pilot man, who walks the track in a special distinctive jacket and establishes that the train may proceed without risk.'

Mr McLellan is gentle and mild-mannered, and has spent forty-two years on the West Highland; in common with many of its station-masters, he is a stickler for neatness and order. There is evidence of spit, polish and elbow grease everywhere, and he himself looked smart enough for church parade. Though his wife, Signalwoman McLellan, a businesslike ex-nurse, was starting a journey to visit friends in Mainz, Germany, on the next Up train, he courteously conducted me around the station premises and patiently answered my questions.

'Life here is not as solitary as it may seem,' he said. 'I'm also the Rannoch postmaster, and people come from all over the moor to collect their pensions, family allowances and so forth; Rannoch School, an outward-bound place like Gordonstoun with its own fire brigade, is only twelve miles away, and we have a lot to do with the lads. They always put on a very fine annual concert; this year they did *The Mikado* and our two girls, Clare and Catherine, sang in the chorus. Then we get the people arriving on the train, landowners like the Duke of Atholl who comes down from Euston on the sleeper and is met here by his chauffeur; the foreign landowners, the Italians and Dutch, usually arrive by helicopter. We also get the lads from the Glasgow Locomotivemen's Angling Club; they've got a hut nearby.'

The drivers come to fish for plump brown trout in Loch Laidon, just a stone's throw from the station and, when time permits, Mr McLellan also goes down with his rod and line to catch something for high tea. But a freshening breeze and cat's paws on the water may send him hurrying home again. One of his many duties is the supervision of the tiny meteorological office located in a

A powdering of snow lies around Rannoch station midway across the moor.

disused station room. He regularly measures rainfall, precipitation, tempera-ture and wind, and enters the figures in his records. As he is living, to all intents and purposes, on the roof of Scotland, the Glasgow Met Office people are keen to know what is going on up there; Mr McLellan spends a good deal of time on the phone telling them. 'I also advise the deer stalkers who pop in to check the strength and direction of the wind,' he says. 'The weather is invariably extreme up here. Just a few days ago, for example, we had 26.8 degrees of frost. It was keen, aye, very keen indeed.'

The station used to be the focal point of the community. Dances, whist drives, even church services were held there; until recently, an organ occupied pride of place in the Rannoch waiting-room, and Mr McLellan still keeps the station Bible – presented in 1918 'for the spiritual benefit . . . of those attending the Church and Mission Services at Rannoch Station' – and a pile of dusty hymn-books locked away in a cupboard. The preacher had to make his own way to Rannoch. The line was always closed on Sundays – and still is. 'Nothing ever moved here on the Sabbath,' Mr McLellan says. 'Even urgent freight had to wait. I grew up at Mallaig, where my father was station foreman, in the days when it was the busiest herring port in Europe. They had steam drifters then, Buckie-registered, and it was all driftnet herring, with also a roaring trade in Queen of Scots kippers from Stornaway; they were the world's finest kippers, eaten by royalty and millionaires, and they were sent off down this line to London and America in bonny stone boxes. But if it was the Sabbath, why, the whole shipment would stay on the Mallaig quay and rot.'

I took my leave and, pulling away from Rannoch's tiny settlement aboard the next train, could see both the Black Mount and Glencoe, framed in steam. We passed the famous snow shed and, at the top of the line, a wooden notice saying 'Corrour Summit 1,350 ft above sea level'. At Corrour itself chickens clucked in the yard and Mr Morgan, the bearded station-master, bustled about in an anorak, plus-fours and crimson moon boots. Though Corrour lies on the edge of the moor it is, if anything, even more solitary and exposed than Rannoch. The nearest neighbour is five miles away and the Morgans' house crouches in the path of the winds like a large boulder.

Mrs Morgan got aboard with three of her four girls. She was going shopping in Fort William while the kids went to school at Roy Bridge. They would return at 4pm in the cab of the afternoon mail train, riding with the driver who, each day, stops especially to pick them up and set them down again. 'They have a nice life,' said Mrs Morgan, a lollipop lady during her husband's previous posting in Fife. 'They've got a donkey, a pony, a dog, a cat and two rabbits.'

'*And* a wee ferret,' said one of the girls, who was about eleven and very pretty; she gave the guard a smouldering look as he went by and the poor man, startled, walked into a door.

'In the summer the lassies have a grocery shop by the station for the youth hostellers,' said Mrs Morgan. 'It's good for their sums. Just occasionally we get hunters coming through as well. The Forestry Commission charges a hundred pounds for a single shot at a deer, hit or miss. But it's a dying sport, shooting,

74

and no joke intended. At Rannoch, once, they had a venison slide going down to the loading bank, so the carcases could be dumped straight on to the train without any fuss. There'd be no call for such a device today.'

We passed a towering wall of granite, the rock neatly pleated, like a kilt. Then, in the Braes o' Lochaber, the River Spean went tumbling wildly through the Monessie Gorge, a stretch of sculpted white stone scoured and chiselled by the whisky-coloured torrent until it was as voluptuous as marble. The girls got off at Roy Bridge and we trundled on past Keppoch House, the ancient seat of the Macdonalds and, not far from Spean Bridge, the memorial to the commandos who had trained nearby during World War II. There were shaggy heifers in the fields and the line was edged by cattle creeps. On the Spean Bridge Up platform an old man took a little water from a metal cup chained to the iron drinking fountain.

We passed Inverlochy Castle and the Long John distillery, set in the looming shadow of Ben Nevis, then ambled up Loch Linnhe to the Fort William station,

The 05.05 evening service for Mallaig leaves the old Fort William station.

798

Fort William Pier & Macbrayne's boat "Fusilier".

The ferry Fusilier *loading passengers at Fort William.*

an undistinguished building not far from the spot where, on 12 February 1692, Colonel Hill took up his quill and signed the order for the Massacre of Glencoe. Beyond, lies the town's single street of shops – many specialising in the supply of shortcake, whisky and tartan – and the first of its numerous churches. The guard, bag packed, flags rolled up and carried rakishly beneath his arm, prepared to leave the train. 'It's been a long morning,' he said. 'I'm ready for a pork pie and a dram of stag's breath.'

They were changing the engine and crew. I had got permission to ride the footplate on to Mallaig and, a few minutes before departure, strolled along the platform to examine the big Class 37 diesel which stood at the head of our three-carriage train, steaming gently. A plate fixed near the door told me that it was an English Electric machine, built at the Vulcan Foundry. The cab was a lofty one, reached by scrambling up a metal ladder, and the driver was already there when I climbed aboard and introduced myself. His name was Hugh MacBeth and he had an extrovert manner, a high colour and a voice accustomed to being heard effortlessly over labouring engines. His son Arnold, the Second Man, was, by contrast, bearded and introspective. I commented on their relationship. 'Aye, it's all family on this line,' said Hugh. 'I've been driving for thirty-nine years – I was the last Mallaig man to qualify in steam – and my father drove on the West Highland before me. Even Arnold's wife works for the railways; she's the carriage cleaner at Mallaig.'

There was an electric hotplate projecting from the bulkhead at my back; a low door opposite led into the nose compartment where they kept a pair of compressors and a motor blower. The engines, visible through a grill at our backs, were massive; even at rest, they throbbed and muttered restlessly. At 10.03, exactly on time, Hugh MacBeth activated them by pulling the long silver throttle-handle towards him.

We began to move, the old 1,750hp diesels barking as we slid away from the shabby municipal graveyard at the end of the platform and on past the Glenlochy distillery to the Mallaig Junction signal-box where Arnold reached out and plucked the token from the hand of a morose signalman. Back on the moor the token had been a heavy iron key. Now it was a shiny brass lozenge attached to a kind of metal horse collar. He hung it from a knob and paused at a swing bridge while a little trawler with an orange funnel completed its descent of Neptune's Staircase – the series of locks which takes the Caledonian Canal up through the Great Glen to Inverness and the sea. Then Hugh MacBeth gunned his engines and moved off down the lochside, past the Wiggins Teape paper mill and the comfortable south-facing houses of Corpach.

Along the shore of Loch Eil there was a tideline of seaweed the colour and texture of hay. After a brief halt at Locheilside we grumbled along a glen with bare hills ascending on one side and a section of swamp down below on the other. Higher up, we ran into a terrific cloudburst. The wipers banged backwards and forwards like beating wings. Spray broke over the windscreen, torrents came off the rocky slopes above and drummed on the roof. The sounds of turbulent water and the odd yawning motion of the locomotive, swaying and dipping along the old line, heightened the illusion of standing in the wheelhouse of a small, stormbound ship.

Hugh MacBeth, peering forward with narrowed eyes, said, 'From time to time you run down stags grazing on the line and anyone willing to take the trouble can make himself a tidy little profit. Antlers are fetching about three pounds a pound at the moment, while the sky's the limit for a good pair of tusks. They turn them into necklaces and they're worth a king's ransom. I know a certain signalman who hacks off the tusks and antlers with a screwdriver kept specially for the purpose. In just one year he made three hundred pounds from the jewellers at Fort William, and took his family off to London on holiday.'

The track led through high, smooth hills, gleaming like copper in the wet. Water continued to sluice off the rock and splash over the train as, steadily, we

A viaduct on the way to Mallaig.

continued our climb towards Glenfinnan and the most famous spot on the line. Diesels thundering, we passed the head of Loch Shiel and crossed the giant concrete viaduct which is aligned, imposingly, like a backdrop behind Bonnie Prince Charlie's absurd monument. A kind of baroque lighthouse with a bearded Jacobite standing gloomily on top, the monument marks the spot where Prince Charles Edward landed from a rowing boat early on the morning of 19 August 1745, a wet Monday, to begin his doomed crusade. Later that day he stood there beneath the dripping pines to watch as William Murray, Duke of Atholl, raised the Stewart Banner and Bishop Hugh MacDonald, Vicar Apostolic of the Highlands, blessed it.

Glenfinnan station is set high on a hillside and surrounded by trees. The rain had stopped as we drew in, but the sound of rushing water was everywhere and Albert Longmore, the signalman in charge, splashed about the platform in wellington boots. He had an eager, boyish manner and wore a blue peaked cap with a nautical cut. 'The trains are all Four-Bellers on this line – that's express passengers,' he told me when I jumped down to say hullo, 'except for the 16.30 mixed Four-One that comes from Fort William on the Down road.' His cosy office contained a coal fire and a comfortable armchair and four framed 'Best-kept Station in Scotland' awards. Standing on the sideboard were a pair of polished, cherished machines, each bearing an engraved plate saying 'Tyler's Patent Train Tablet Apparatus'; the tokens they contained were fashioned from the best copper brass and, worn smooth by generations of handling, as sleek and heavy as jade.

Hugh MacBeth, pulling away up the incline, told me about a Glenfinnan station-master who had bred whippets. 'I was driving Bantam Cocks then,' said Hugh, 'and the freights coming from Mallaig were loaded with only one thing: herring. It leaked through the floorboards and down on to the line, making the train slip and slide all over the place. Dreadful, it was. Anyway, one morning this chap stopped us at Glenfinnan and said he wanted some herring for his dogs. I told him to help himself. He struggled with a wagon door for a few minutes and jerked it open and maybe, och, I dunno, ten ton of wet fish poured out on to the platform and buried him.'

Albert Longmore, signalman in charge of Glenfinnan station. His cosy office contained four 'Best-kept Station in Scotland' awards.

A small viaduct at Morar.

We slid through those moist brown uplands towards Loch Eilt. The long fingers of snow lying high on the rock faces became suddenly noisy and animated as we went by; they turned out to be burns furiously in spate. A heron took up station in front of us and, legs trailing, led us on down the line with a measured, steady beat of its wings. In Loch Eilt there were tiny islands planted with tall trees, each atoll standing precariously in the glassy water, balanced on its own reflection.

The sun came out for a moment and we climbed back into a dazzling prospect of hills, all glowing in the lovely tawny Highland light, and creaked to a halt at Lochailort where the station building, though abandoned and boarded up, is as elegant as a small cricket pavilion. It stood beside a white picket fence and a row of fine trees and was the site, during the line's construction at the turn of the century, of one of the largest of the navvies' camps. There were two thousand workers based at Lochailort, many of them local men; hereabouts the crofters themselves helped lay the rails, chairs, spikes, fish plates and Scots fir sleepers. 'Excellent rockmen,' said a contemporary report. 'Frugal, living mostly on oatmeal.' They used their shovels for cooking, polishing them like silver spoons after use in both the fire and the clay.

There was now a discernible whiff of salt in the air and, a few minutes later, as we weaved in and out of a series of brief tunnels, I glimpsed the sea frothing around the rocks far below. We crossed a bridge fashioned from concrete but tricked out with phoney battlements to gratify the whim of a local landowner and, approaching Arisaig, saw the island of Rhum and the Scuir of Eigg standing massively on the horizon. Then came a forest full of petrified trees hung with creepers like pale green ribbons and, soon afterwards, mossy copses of pines as formal as Japanese gardens.

There were, Hugh told me, five drivers based at Mallaig; once there had been a dozen. 'We used to have a young lady traction trainee here as well,' he said, 'but she's gone to Cricklewood. She was all right, that lass, not a bad driver at all; her only drawback was she couldn't spend a penny out the door like the lads do.'

He hummed to himself as we motored on up the coast then, outside Morar, halted at a sign saying 'STOP – Open Crossing Gates Before Proceeding'. That was a job for Arnold, the Second Man, who grabbed the key and hopped down to the track. As his father cautiously took the train over the street and into the station, Arnold chatted to a thin, earnest woman who had emerged from a small building with the single word SHOP painted on it.

'We've got a monster here in Loch Morar, you know,' Hugh said to me. 'That one up in Loch Ness may get all the publicity, but this one is a better monster in every respect. If you want to see it all you've got to do is drink a few large scotches on an empty stomach. A few more and it'll come and sit at the bar and tell you jokes.'

The line climbs past Morar's municipal cemetery, set on a hillside, and then begins its descent into Mallaig, trundling past a beached trawler and a deserted slipway. The tide was rising, and the Sound of Sleat seemed to be swishing

The Mallaig pier was an important departure point for Skye.

around our wheels. The station is built of grey stone and has a high, stout wall protecting its platforms from the winds. The platform gardens looked like untended graves. I said goodbye to Hugh and wandered off to explore the village.

Later, when night was starting to fall, I walked down to the quay. The last herring boats were coming in, towing clouds of screaming gulls behind them. Skye loomed darkly over the water. In the harbour a seal swam slowly about, blowing audibly, periodically turning over to float on its back and stare reflectively up at the first stars. As I made my way to the Marine Hotel, looking forward to a bath and a drink and fresh fish for tea, Hugh MacBeth was preparing to take the train back through the shadowy glens to Fort William. Clouds of steam boiled up over the station roof while, out on the islands, the lights were coming on.

Slowly by the
wild Welsh waters

DOVEY JUNCTION TO PWLLHELI

One of the oddest aspects of the railway journey from Dovey Junction to Pwllheli is that your train can be delayed by heavy seas. At the Dovey Junction box, signalman H. R. Hughes tries to anticipate the weather, monitoring the occluded fronts coming in from the Atlantic and keeping his well-thumbed copy of *Laver's Liverpool Tide Tables* constantly to hand. The box, from which he controls distant signals in no less than three counties, stands in a marsh at the head of a broad estuary and is reached by following a mile-long duck-hunters' track through the reeds – the only access to the junction for those not travelling by train. When he arrives there he sniffs the wind and casts an eye over the estuary. 'If the tide's over thirty foot and there's a stiff westerly whipping up the white horses it means you're in for a real swamper,' he told me, 'specially if the moon's new or full.'

The River Dovey runs close by and salmon are netted within a few yards of the platform. Here the permanent way divides and sets off on either side of the bay, one line going to Aberystwyth, a twenty-six-mile run of no particular consequence, the other beginning its tortuous 53½-mile journey around the exposed and windy coast of Cardigan Bay to the little port of Pwllheli. H. R. Hughes's box, the most important on the line, is equipped with tall iron levers against which he tends to lean during the long waits between trains, allowing them to support his comfortable frame while, through the large plate-glass windows, he ponders the slow changing of the seasons.

I visited him one morning when a chill spring wind was sweeping across the estuary, and he remarked that one would never imagine it was only a month until the first cuckoo was due. 'Last year it sang on April 21,' he said. 'Always around the middle of April the drivers begin stopping and asking if I've heard it yet; when, finally, I say yes, the news goes straight up the line – the Dovey cuckoo is back. My own attitude towards cuckoos is this: it's always nice to see them again, but they're very fond of the sound of their own voices and on long summer nights they can send you bloody barmy, can't they? One evening last year there were *three* of them out here on the telephone wires, all singing so loud I had to chuck stones at them for a bit of quiet.'

A companionable silence fell between us as, propped against his levers, H. R. Hughes gazed contemplatively out at the estuary. He had a gentle manner and the sleek, clerky look of the well-fed indoor worker though, within minutes, I was to find that there was more to him than met the eye. Now I noted that the

A stretch of line at low tide.

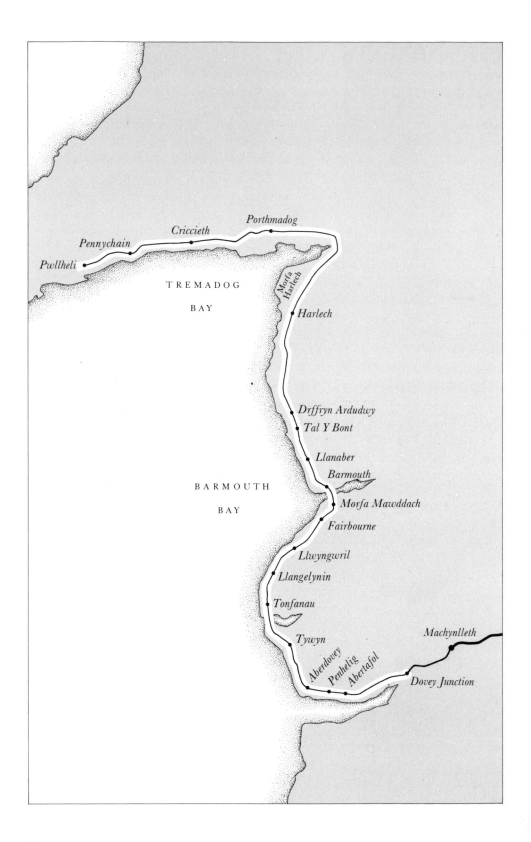

estuary seemed full of breaking waves and all around us the marsh was beginning to stir. Glittering in the thin sun, the overflow eddied towards us, tugging at the reeds and then spilling over the rails. 'The sea's coming on to your track,' I said.

'Often does that,' he replied, unconcerned. 'In a quarter of an hour it will be high tide, see, and the wind is dead behind it. But this is nothing. You should have been around on the evening of 2 January 1976, the night we had the tidal wave. About 8 pm there was a terrible roar in the west and half the Irish Sea suddenly fell out of the sky. I remember seeing the Gents down there on the platform go under like a U-boat venting its tanks and then the water started climbing up my windows and I thought to myself, "Put your coat on, Hughes, it's time to go home." I rapped out the Section Obstructed signal – six beats on my bell – then pulled all the signals on to Stop and set off, on hands and knees, along the Aberystwyth metals which lead up there to the safety of that hillside. It took an hour to cover one mile, going from sleeper to sleeper, pulling myself along the rails, hand over hand, while the undertow tugged and these fantastic waves kept racing in and breaking about my ears. It was like Waikiki Beach out there and next day, when it had all subsided, I saw that the trackbed had been scooped out like a melon while the rails were all ripped up and as twisted as paper clips.'

Bells rang and signal levers were thrown. A train approached, a little two-car diesel bound for Pwllheli and driven by a round-shouldered, shaggy-haired man in a tweed cap and a sweater emblazoned with a brewery crest. It set off cautiously across the small lake which now surrounded the box, its reflection trembling wildly then slipping out of focus in the ripples made by its wheels. Back on dry land, it rattled away through the reeds as H. R. Hughes began preparing for the arrival of the train I was planning to catch up the valley to Machynlleth. Watching him, I asked whether pulling the levers needed much effort. He invited me to try the one controlling the solitary Distant standing against the skyline a mile up the Aberystwyth track. 'But don't snatch,' he said. 'If the wire snaps you'll go through the window like a howitzer shell.'

I strained at the lever as if my life depended on it. I hauled and heaved and shoved and grunted but the old semaphore, seen through an increasingly red haze, didn't budge. 'It's jammed,' I gasped, and H. R. Hughes permitted himself a faint smile. He seized the lever in both hands and embraced it like a dancing partner; then, as though launching into a classical tango, he suddenly dipped from the waist and threw himself across the room. The lever crashed into the Go position while, far away across the marsh, the signal dropped to its lower quadrant. When my train drew in I said goodbye with deep respect, reflecting on the hitherto unsuspected fact that rural signalmen need the strength of lumberjacks. Twenty minutes later, pulling into Machynlleth, I noted the signalman there idly watching us from his box, mug of tea in hand. He was a homely grey-haired figure in spectacles and a cardigan and, as I walked along the Down platform with its worn slate-fronted letterbox – inscribed with the letters VR – I imagined him driving home each evening to tear up

The rising tide creeps over the track at Dovey Junction.

telephone directories and bend crowbars for the amusement of his grand-children.

The office of the traffic manager, or rheolwr trafnidiaeth, had institutional mustard walls and smelt of paper, ink and old copper coins. The station's *Accident Register* was lying on a desk and I opened it, noting that in 1953 a platelayer named P. P. Jones had been kicked below the left knee by a cow, while L. S. Williams, a porter, had fallen off a table while winding the station clock. The door opened and Christine Taylor walked in. An honours graduate in philosophy and mathematics from the University of Kent, she was the first female traffic manager employed on the Welsh railways and, at twenty-two, also one of the youngest. A dark-haired, dark-eyed English girl whose father worked for Rolls-Royce in Bristol, she controlled the working lives of fifty men, many of whom seem to be named Jones. Her manner was composed and friendly, but a trace of iron entered her voice when someone brought in a grubby uniform cap which had been blown off a guard's head and recovered by

88

a member of the public. Miss Taylor indicated that she knew all about this guard. He had been losing his cap for years, apparently never comprehending that if you leant from a speeding train the slipstream was likely to remove any headgear not secured by a chin strap. Miss Taylor planned to have a chat with him. She asked the booking clerk to make tea and then sat at her desk and enumerated her duties.

'There are five signal-boxes on my section, and I must inspect one a week,' she said. 'Also I have to test my fifteen signalmen every two years on rules, regulations and procedures. I'm responsible for the fifteen drivers and eleven guards at the Train Crew Depot here, and I must prepare their rosters, bearing in mind matters like the thirty-minute "physical needs break" they must have between the third and fifth hours, and local peculiarities like our two brothers who hate each other so much they won't speak; though they don't allow personal feelings to interfere with their duties, when either requires a Second Man I must nevertheless make a point of not rostering them together. I'm in

Mr H. R. Hughes, Dovey Junction signalman. Through the windows he ponders the slow changing of the seasons.

89

The Machynlleth engine shed, seen here in the Sixties, is the size of a village church.

BELOW
Christine Taylor at Machynlleth. The first female traffic manager on the Welsh railways, she controls the working lives of fifty men.

charge of the booking office and also responsible for every first-aid box and fire extinguisher on my patch. I must check all the detonators and, each week, visit all the open crossings and test the telephones.'

Miss Taylor displayed a lively interest in local railway history and, while waiting for my train, showed me a cupboard stacked with musty bundles of Great Western stationery, including hundreds of yellowing forms for reporting 'Collisions, Derailments, Fires on Trains and at Stations, Floods and Land-slips'. (Fires on Embankments were to be reported by the Engineering Department on Form 1051.) When my little diesel came in I said goodbye to Miss Taylor and went rolling back down the long green valley to Dovey Junction. There the driver, observing the rules for the operation of single-track railways, collected a silver token from H. R. Hughes. Having traversed the flood and left a wake that sucked and splashed at the surrounding reeds, we set off over oak sleepers for the weathered wooden bridge spanning the river.

The track wound along the base of a steep cliff and beside a flinty foreshore. Pink crabs were sunning themselves by the rockpools as we ducked through a series of tunnels and on past the remote halt at Abertafol, a rickety timber structure set in a wilderness of rushes beside the estuary. An old man was sitting opposite me. He had a toothless, sunken face and glasses so thick they seemed fashioned from the bases of milk bottles; their opacity made his eyes enormous and disembodied, like fish in a tank. 'The only people they'll pick up here are

90

summer walkers wanting a ride into Aberdovey or Tywyn,' he remarked. 'There was a guard pre-war who grumbled about it, because the few pennies he got for the tickets didn't cover the cost of the stop in coal and wear on the brake shoes. It's no good to you, that kind of traffic, you see.'

Penhelig, set between two curving tunnels and seen from a lofty wooden halt, is a steep village of ascending planes and acute angles. Around Aberdovey there are dunes and, running between the line and the beach, a golf course. At Tywyn the track snakes back to the sea, though the two are segregated by a barricade of massive boulders and concrete blocks positioned to offer protection from the fury of Atlantic storms. Now the westerly that had flooded Dovey was whipping up the spring tide and spattering the train with froth. A permanent way gang dressed in dripping orange oilskins eyed us morosely as we motored by but then, suddenly, we were climbing, looking down through our streaming windows at the lumpy seas below.

The Ffriog cliff with its avalanche shelter.

The once-busy station at Tonfanau is semi-derelict today.

My companion noted that we were passing the grassy halt of Tonfanau. 'Last year nobody got off there *at all*,' he said. 'Two people apparently got on, though. Dunno who they were, but there was a lot of talk about it down the line.' We were traversing a hillside squared off by drystone walls. It was arid, salty country inhabited only by a few black-faced sheep whose thick fleeces flapped raggedly in the wind. Soon afterwards the line began its cautious approach to the Ffriog, the notorious section where the track runs along a ledge cut into the side of a cliff. It was here, on 4 March 1933, that a rockfall caused the engine of the early morning mail from Machynlleth to spin off the rails and tumble on to the boulders a hundred feet below; its single carriage, a converted Dean clerestory with its dining alcoves and first-class dog lockers removed for service on the coast, remained sitting intact on the track. When the rising tide began to lap around the mangled wreckage of the locomotive, the smallest railwayman in the salvage party, a ganger named W. A. Spoonley, was ordered to crawl into the crushed cab to extract the remains of the driver and fireman. The official with the green lamp who had daily walked the line before the first train came through, and who had been fired as an economy measure, was promptly reinstated.

A railway avalanche shelter stands on the spot like a solitary alpine chapel and, as we passed beneath its sturdy ecclesiastical buttresses, I reflected that

The engine which fell from the Ffriog in 1933.

Builders at work last century on the Cambrian Coast line.

only the Victorians would have had the effrontery to run a line along the face of a cliff as sheer as this one. The parapet beside the track was lined with gulls which lazily spread their wings and spilled off as we came past, floating out over the abyss and then sliding back when we had gone. We began our descent, still accompanied by that rippling wave of white pinions, and then swung away from the shore and headed across gorse-lined fields into Fairbourne, a resort with an audible level crossing signal that moaned like a wounded animal. Past Morfa Mawddach we slowed almost to walking pace to cross the half-mile-long timber Barmouth viaduct. Once it had been able to accommodate all the standard Cambrian coast locos – the little Metro tanks, the Barnums, Stellas and Dukes, the ubiquitous Dean Goods, the Large Sharp Stewarts and Small Sharp Stewarts, the Peacocks and Bulldogs, Manors and Moguls. Now, though, because the wooden piles were riddled internally by a voracious marine borer and externally by a species of sea louse called the gribble worm, traffic was restricted to the little lightweight diesel units in which I was now riding.

As we rumbled slowly out over the Mawddach estuary, my friend remarked: 'When Benjamin Piercy built this viaduct in 1867 there was a man over at Barmouth who promised that if they ever finished it he would eat the first train to come over. The morning it was due a table was laid outside Barmouth with a starched white cloth and the best silver, wasn't it, and as the train approached the chairman of the railway turned to this fellow and said, "Here it comes now. Do you want it boiled or fried?"' He laughed so hard that he seemed to collapse,

A train moves carefully over the worm-infested Barmouth viaduct.

95

shaking, in upon himself. As I peered over the gunmetal water towards the Clogau mines from which, traditionally, gold is extracted for the Royal Family's wedding rings, my friend wiped his eyes with the cuff of his coat and lapsed into silence.

We rolled over the roof of the lifeboat house and into a pretty little town whose prosperity was founded on flannel and hosiery. The sea at its front had inhibited its expansion in a way that the towering cliff at its back has not; set among the houses which go scrambling up the rockface is the massive church of St John, paid for by Mrs Dyson Perrins with her Worcester Sauce fortune and suspended so high that on Sabbath nights its illuminated windows must have served as supplementary beacons for 'the hundred small sloops' the community once possessed.

Alighting at the handsome station by the beach, I met a bulky, beaming figure who wore his cap with the peak sticking out over his right ear and a uniform jacket several sizes too small for him. This was Gwynn Jones, the legendary Barmouth lamp man. It was he who attended to the lights that still burn on top of the old Great Western signal posts – each crowned with the kind of spiky ornamentation once found on Prussian helmets – filling them with paraffin, cleaning, trimming and tending them. Though he has been promoted to porter and his duties taken over by a monosyllabic young man named Bruce, he remains universally known as Gwynn the Wick or, if you prefer it, simply as The Wick. 'Want a cup of tea, boyo?' The Wick asked me. 'Lord Harlech is relief clerk today and he's got the kettle on in the booking office.'

Indoors I met a plump, dapper man in a red bow tie who explained that the lads had ennobled him because he talked a bit posh and, now and then, liked a round of golf at the Royal St David's. The Harlech reference was a tacit recognition of the part the family had played in the local railway system; he lived with his father in the Harlech station house, and both his father and grandfather had held the post of Harlech station-master. His real name is Len Humphries. 'When my dad was still just a youngster,' he explained in his patrician voice, 'the *real* Lord Harlech used the railway telegraph system to get his Stock Exchange information. He always gave my father, who earned 3s 6d a week on the railways, sixpence for delivering it to him by hand. The station-master took half as a kind of commission and then, regular as clockwork, nipped up to the Ship Aground with his threepence for twenty Capstans and a pint of wallop.' From his wallet he produced a pile of snapshots of the Royal Jubilee visit to Harlech. There were shots of the Royal Train, the carriages as lustrous as Oriental lacquerwork, and several studies of the Royal luggage. 'Do you know what the Queen's got written on her labels?' he said to me. I shook my head. '"The Queen",' he said. 'Not many of the gricers noticed that.' As the next service for Pwllheli pulled out of the sanctuary of the station, the guard, a friendly, personable man named A. B. Jones, told me that 'gricer' was railway parlance for train enthusiast.

I noted that, once clear of the town, we were again at the whim of a playful sea. Wave after wave came skidding up the beach and over the track, striking us with a moist thump and making the sunlight opaque as they broke across the windows. The driver, hunched behind his flailing windscreen wiper, did not look happy, but at least he was better off than the people who had manned the steam locomotives before him. Hereabouts was the point where the sea often sloshed into the open footplates, soaking the drivers and firemen to the skin; probably more profanities had been uttered over this brief stretch of coastline than on any other comparable fragment of the British Isles.

At Llanaber there is a small thirteenth-century church with a graveyard full of dead sailors. The Tal Y Bont halt consists of a footbridge, a lone tree and a mysterious sign warning train drivers to beware of trains, while at Dyffryn Ardudwy there is a pretty country pub and the remains of countless Stone Age cairns, forts and granite circles. And everywhere, like the flowers of an insidious fungoid growth, one sees the creeping colonies of caravans. Harlech was first glimpsed around the lee of a hill. It stands, massive and distinguished, before a huge reach of beach which, when the tide is out and there isn't 20–20 cloud cover, reflects the blueness of the sky in such a remarkable way that the township seems set beside several hundred acres of gleaming Delft porcelain. The mossy greens of the Royal St David's Golf Club – where Lloyd George and the Prince of Wales battled against the sea winds – lie at the base of the rock and close to the celebrated castle.

The station is built down at the bottom, too, not far from the castle entrance known as the Water Gate. I was admiring the neat dove-grey station house where Lord Len, the relief clerk, lived with his father, when the train tilted sharply as a regiment of schoolchildren came aboard. 'We carry five hundred kids up and down the line every day,' said A. B. Jones without enthusiasm. 'Apart from the seasonal summer visitors, they're our main source of income.' Several youngsters clambered into the luggage racks to sleep while, down below, sporadic fighting broke out. A. B. Jones sighed and went to instil a bit of order.

We crossed Morfa Harlech, a kind of savanna over which the line runs as straight as an arrow. Later, there were glimpses up into the Vale of Ffestiniog and, across a pretty estuary, of the elegant Italianate buildings erected by Sir Clough Williams-Ellis at Portmeirion. In the fields lambs scampered wildly about on their stiff, splayed legs as we came by. A week before, someone said, a driver had seen a ewe caught in a bramble hedge. The next day it was still there so he stopped the train and, leaving his passengers to their own devices, climbed down and marched away across the fields to set it free, thus demonstrating the priorities of many of the people who man the rural railways.

Near Glaslyn there were stupendous views of marshes, bays and islands, with Snowdon in the background, and then the line took us across an extensive bog into Porthmadog, a neat and prosperous little town which once shipped its best-quality slate all over the world. One remnant of that period is Ballast Island at the mouth of the port, an atoll made from basalt, tuff, schist, granite, reef skerry and other rocks brought in the holds of the inbound vessels and thrown overboard when they dropped anchor. Porthmadog station, with its deep, shadowy platform veranda and blue iron pillars, looks like a stylish Australian squatters' residence: travellers entering the station house to enquire about fares or departure times tend to remain indoors for some time, glass in hand as they happily ponder the fact that the place has been turned into a pub.

The line, now almost at the end of its run, goes rollicking through woods and green hills towards Criccieth, where there is a thirteenth-century castle built by the princes of Gwynedd and later occupied by both Edward 1 and Owen Glendower. Criccieth is the Victorian resort town where Lloyd George and his brother William had their law practice. For fifty-four years it was also part of David Lloyd George's Parliamentary constituency, and even when Churchill — who always regarded him as the greatest Welshman since the time of the Tudors — tried to tempt him out of retirement by offering him the Washington embassy, he preferred to stay where he was. He died at Criccieth, and his body was placed on a horse-drawn farmer's cart and taken up the road to Llanystumdwy; that was where he had grown up and it was there, beside the River Dwyfor, that he was buried. Mrs A. A. Jones remembers the great man walking about Criccieth. 'He had long white hair and in the summer was as brown as a nut; the holidaymakers always loved to catch a glimpse of him.'

Mrs Jones is a small, exuberant woman of seventy who lives in a tiny yellow cottage beside one of Criccieth's two level crossings. She operates one set of main gates, a set of wicket gates and a signal, and has been controlling the crossing all her working life. The most significant advance for her during that period was the invention of the lightweight metal gate. 'The old wooden ones were heavy even on a windless day,' she recalls. 'When there was a strong westerly blowing you needed all your strength to move them.' Hard by the crossing is a tiny cabin, no larger than a sentry box, which contains four gleaming levers. One operates the signal, one locks the main gates, one locks the Up wicket and the other the Down wicket. 'As soon as the Up train starts off Mrs N. Jones at the Pwllheli crossing gives me one long ring on the big bell to tell me it's on its way and that I've got fifteen minutes. It also rings at Mrs Williams's, her down at the bottom, at the other Criccieth crossing. She then changes a signal four hundred yards from her box, which is a very long pull for a woman her age.'

The final segment of my journey, the brief run to Pwllheli, took me through fields and past the Butlins holiday camp cantonment at Penychain, the gaudily painted longhouse accommodation units making it look like the kind of place vacationing Dyaks might favour. 'I remember coming past here just after some thieves had dropped the proceeds of a robbery,' said A. B. Jones. 'There were pound notes blowing in our slipstream like falling leaves and silver from the one-armed bandits glittering right up the track.' Moments later we passed the Pwllheli engine shed, now converted and bearing a sign saying Menai Handy Foods, and pulled into the tumbledown terminus. The train had passed through twenty-nine stations and maintained an average speed of twenty-seven miles an hour, making it — allegedly — the slowest service in Britain.

Steam Safari
up the Valley

ABERYSTWYTH TO DEVIL'S BRIDGE

Every morning in season, Trevor Davies picks up his matches and walks through the Aberystwyth shed to begin firing up. He is British Rail's only practising steam raiser, and his three venerable little tank engines operate the last steam service on the national network. Thirty years ago there were well over twenty-two thousand steam locomotives in the British Railways fleet; hardly a corner of the kingdom did not lie within earshot of a branch line, and the breathy whoop of a passing Black Five's steam trumpet was as much a sound of the countryside as the cawing of rooks or the striking of the church clock. Mr Davies's steamers, the last in British public ownership, work the 11¾-mile narrow gauge line from Aberystwyth up the Vale of Rheidol to the solitary hamlet of Devil's Bridge, and they are midgets, a mere twenty-two-feet long measured over the buffer beams.

Outside the Aberystwyth engine shed.

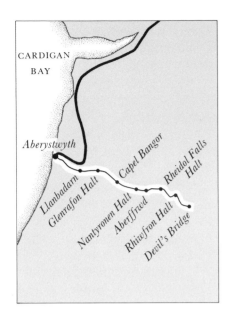

Like the legions of steam raisers before him who got the country moving each morning, Mr Davies requires the patience of Job. From a cold start, it takes about three hours to raise a decent head of steam. He uses the shutdown process, evolved to avoid thermal cracking of the boiler, which means popping a piece of burning cotton waste through the firebox door and turning on the fuel (diesel oil since the engines were converted at Swindon) for five minutes. Then the fuel is switched off and the fire extinguished for a further five minutes. The process is repeated for ten, fifteen and finally twenty minutes when, at some time during the burn, there should be movement on the steam gauge. The engine can then be left to bubble and simmer for the couple of hours it will need to reach the 165lb pressure necessary for operating up the Himalayan gradients that lie in wait on the road to Devil's Bridge.

It is during this period that Robert John Davies arrives, walking along the 23½ gauge track from the station a couple of hundred yards away. He is one of the nine Aberystwyth footplate men qualified to drive steam locomotives, and he had been rostered to work the 14.15 service on which, one glorious April afternoon, I planned to travel.

It would be hauled by the locomotive *Owain Glyndwr*, built by the Great Western Railway at Swindon in 1923. 'Good little engine, that one,' Mr Davies remarked, nodding at it. 'Free steaming and very responsive, very free on the boxes. She'll run with just a breath of steam, just walk away with you.' He began checking the locomotive before accepting responsibility for it, moving around it with the ease of long familiarity. A stocky, white-haired man with pink cheeks, shy eyes and a gentle, unassertive manner, he had joined the railways forty-seven years earlier, working as a greaser at Machynlleth, up the Dovey valley. He had known the *Owain Glyndwr* when she ran under Great Western colours and later, after nationalisation in 1948, was painted mainline green and emblazoned with the famous lion-and-wheel emblem.

Mr Davies, an old-fashioned driver who works by the book, examined everything from the condition of the fire to his water gauges and fusible plugs. Before it had its boiler reconditioned, he would also have checked that the lumps of Welsh steam coal were no larger than a man's fist and distributed evenly and sparsely across the grate. (Too much coal on the fire made your smoke yellow.)

Leaving him peering into his sandboxes, I went to explore the shed. It had a lofty, steeply pitched roof and was as large as a church. The three little engines stood gleaming in the shadows. The *Llywelyn*, painted black, was steaming too, fired-up by order of the Board of Trade which has decreed that a stand-by engine must always be held in readiness during operations. Nearby, the *Prince of Wales*, coloured a kind of tobacco brown and bearing the emblem of the original Vale of Rheidol Light Railway Company, had the lustre of richly waxed wood; the engine's brasswork glinted like newly minted sovereigns. Down among the wheels and the shadowy jumble of pistons, rods, valves, rocker shafts, sheaves, eccentrics, cranks, trunnion pins and gudgeon pins that constituted the driving mechanisms, jets of steam hissed and spat, leaving warm, moist patches on my trousers as I wandered past.

102

The tank engine Edward VII with footplate crew.

At 13.45 Mr Davies settled his ancient cap on his head and swung himself up on to the footplate. He had signed his Route Knowledge Card twenty-three years earlier and now, accompanied by an intense, dark-haired young fireman, he took the regulator handle in his left hand and the reversing lever in the right. With a volcanic rush of steam and smoke we backed slowly out of the shed, up the line to the station and the old Carmarthen branch platform, modified to take narrow gauge trains. Nearby was the curious little Vale of Rheidol Ground Frame, four uncovered levers which control several sets of points and the only signal left on the line – a solitary Home. A stern notice on the frame said, 'Train Spotters Must Not Pass Beyond This Point.'

Four carriages and a sizeable crowd awaited us. Two of the carriages were open and two closed, each accommodating about fifty people on hard pine benches. (In 1905 they had briefly introduced miniature first-class carriages, sumptuously fitted out with padded leather seats, carpeted floors, steam heating and, for night services, ceiling lamps made from pots of burning colza oil.) Mr Davies scrambled down and went to fetch his staff. This is a single track line, and drivers must have in their possession the iron staff or heavy brass ticket that can only be issued by the Aberystwyth supervisor or, at the other end, by Norman Simkins, the Devil's Bridge Person-in-Charge.

I remained on the footplate, observing the enthusiasts who stood around sniffing the steam as joyously as hounds scenting a hare. While their children surveyed the train politely and took a few desultory pictures with their Instamatics, they spoke intensely to each other of gland nuts and stuffing boxes, poppet valves and grease nipples, rocking grates and motion parts, mudhole doors, steam fountains and Caprotti valve gear. One enthusiast, elderly, lean

On the way to Devil's Bridge.

and magisterial, said, 'Arthur was shed staff pre-war. Definitely. It was post-war that he drove, finishing up on the old Drummonds, I believe. You used to get dirty ankles on them, due to the way the coal dust swirled about your boots.' And a small, gregarious man wearing rimless spectacles spoke bossily to a companion. 'No, it's the cavity under the *small* air clack,' he said. 'Your large air clack stays shut and the main air clack is closed by the bell crank. See?'

'Yus,' said his companion sullenly.

Mr Davies returned bearing his staff and, with fifteen minutes to go, relaxed against the rear wall of the cab and told me he drove the Vale of Rheidol every second week; the rest of the time he operated the little Cambrian Coast diesels from Aberystwyth up to Shrewsbury and back – and he despised them. 'There's nothing about those DMUs that recommends them to a driver,' he said in his soft, quick voice. 'Steam has the capacity, see, to let a driver display his talents, even show off a little. It brings out the best in a man. The power you had there! It was like controlling a waterfall, or a volcano. And, of course, steamers hardly ever let you down, they usually got you home. You can thrash a steamer if you have to and it will respond, even if its at the end of its tether, but that doesn't work with diesels. When there's some problem with a diesel it just stops and goes out, like a light bulb.'

The enthusiasts standing around the *Owain Glyndwr* scowled up at me, resenting my presence on the footplate, jealous of the way Mr Davies was taking me into his confidence and bestowing friendship and favours upon me. They strained to listen as he explained the various controls. 'The regulator, there, is your throttle and the reversing lever, here, your gears. These two things up here work the whistles. The driver has a high-tone whistle for long-distance work – perhaps to warn a distant station that he's approaching – while the fireman has a low-frequency, close-quarter whistle he'd use to scare cows off an unmanned crossing. That pair of levers is for sanding. They activate sandpipes at the back and the front, the leaders and trailers, through which we deliver a special fire-dried sand on to the rails. And that down there is the firehole door.'

Often the motion of the locomotive was so violent that the fireman had to work on his knees. And invariably, he worked under the driver's supervision. 'You wouldn't let him put coal just anywhere,' said Mr Davies. 'To keep the steam gauge on its red running mark you would *specify*, wouldn't you, telling him to feed the front of the fire or feed the back. The fire burned sweetest when the nuggets were spread evenly; and if there were any holes or thin spots you filled them, often placing the lumps by hand. "Little and often" was the maxim when it came to shovelling coal but, in the end, it all depends on the driver's skill. I recall one chap, a real slogger, who would shove his shoulder under the regulator and leave it there for the duration of the journey, just sitting puffing at his pipe and staring straight ahead and not giving a toss how much coal he burnt. You met quite a few like that and they made life very hard for their firemen. On the other hand, you'd get a driver like one I fired for at Machynlleth, the finest driver I ever knew, whose attitude towards wasting coal was that it was a mortal sin. He never made smoke or blew off steam, and he'd only let you build up the fire a few moments before departure. He was a perfectionist, that chap; if he found a single piece of clinker on his footplate he'd be dancing. But what a driver! He could get a loco moving with just a following wind.'

It was time to be off. Mr Davies gave a sharp blast on his whistle and the enthusiasts hastened back to board the carriages. With a terrific rush of steam and the clamour of straining pistons we began to move, smoke pouring from the copper-rimmed chimney and breaking up to drift away through the spring sunshine like small rainclouds. We left the engine shed behind us and headed through an industrial estate containing the premises of Emco Carpets, Ideal Bread and Keen Cost Cash and Carry. There was nobody at the Llanbadarn halt, which only gets busy during the period of the local agricultural show. Then a shuttle service is laid on into Aberystwyth and the little carriages are crowded with taciturn Welsh farmers down from the hills in their flat caps and shiny Sunday suits. All that remains of the station complex is a corrugated-iron shed in which they may shelter from the rain.

We rattled through playing fields and past a sign restricting Mr Davies to a speed of ten miles an hour. There was a level crossing with cars banked up behind the barriers, the locals looking peeved at having been caught by a toy train that – this early in the season – only passed twice a day, the visitors springing out and fumbling with their cameras as we chugged by, their faces suffused with pleasure. It was not a happiness I altogether shared, since the footplate of a steam locomotive is a pretty uncomfortable place to be. First, the noise was terrible. The burners roared and thundered, there was the sustained metronomic thump of loose valve control gear, strident as an empty oil drum being rapidly struck with a cricket stump, while the whistles made a noise close to the threshold of pain. Second, space was severely restricted. The footplate was only slightly roomier than a telephone kiosk and, to ensure that I didn't get in the crew's way, I stood pressed up against the rear wall, clinging to a length of warm piping. Third, the ride was rougher than an unsprung bullock cart crossing a field of stubble. The bends were especially turbulent, the wheel flanges banging against the rails, squealing and straining and making the *Owain Glyndwr* tremble and sway.

I mentioned the unsteadiness to Mr Davies, who looked surprised. He thought, clearly, that we were having a remarkably smooth run. 'You should have tried some of the big steamers,' he shouted over his shoulder. 'They *rolled*. They began rolling the moment you started off and they kept rolling until you stopped – except when you hit a rough patch. Then they jumped up and down.'

We bumped and clattered on over a marsh and the flimsy timber bridge spanning the Rheidol, its water the colour of black tea. A heron took up station beside the engine and escorted us across the flood plain of the Rheidol to Glen-rafon Halt before peeling away in the direction of the heronry on the Ystwyth. In the meadows sheep grazed among the buttercups and oxeye daisies; earlier a shepherdess had told me that the foxes, just then, were killing record numbers of lambs; first thing each morning she went around in the Land-Rover

Aberffrwd station with staff. The antique Nelson stove at which they warmed themselves is still there.

At Aberffrwd today the train pauses to take on water.

and counted the night's tally of victims, disembowelled by the predators or left with their throats torn out. Along the valley floor the wild fruit trees were in blossom, the scents of apple, cherry and plum drifting fragrantly through the oily confines of the footplate. Near Pwllcenamon Farm the line passes a river bend where young sand-martins tumbled like autumn leaves above the loop of water. As we drew away a solitary kingfisher came past, incandescent, heading west, going like a tiny comet.

At Capel Bangor, where the Vale of Rheidol carriages used to be shedded, nine Pease levers set in a ground frame once controlled the points and signals; each autumn the arms of the signals were dismantled and locked away in an Aberystwyth cupboard to stop rabbit hunters taking pot shots at them with their Webleys. Now there is nothing at Capel Bangor at all, and the stop is significant merely for the fact that it stands at the beginning of the first gradient. The engine note deepened and quickened as we banged and lurched up an incline to a lofty river terrace and then climbed on to Nantyronen Halt, once a busy little station with a Vale of Rheidol company cottage set in trees behind the siding; only the name board remains today.

We pressed on. There was dogwood and wild mustard on either side of the line and, at Aberffrwd, rhododendrons. We paused there to take on water, five

hundred gallons pumped from the Nant yr Aber by a hydram water hammer, a revolutionary Victorian device worked entirely by the push of the underground stream. I hopped down and wandered into the remains of the little corrugated-iron booking office. In a corner stood a rusting Nelson stove, once used to warm the clerk as he supervised the parcel traffic (bronze figures, felt hats, marble clocks, clay pipes, symphoniums, ship's compasses and magic lantern slides were among the articles Carried at Owner's Risk) and sold his twopenny tickets to Aber. It was extraordinarily peaceful. Bees hummed and the sleepy splash of a nearby creek acted as a counterpoint to the small, wheezing noises of the engine at rest. Green shoots sprouted along the track, springing up between the worn sleepers. I asked the earnest young fireman, who sat smoking in the sun, what they were. 'Oh, just weeds, I would think, wouldn't you?' he said. A pretty blonde girl in a blue dress told him they looked like baby marijuana plants, and he gave her an uncertain smile. A few yards down the hill there was a dark, prim church and a graveyard full of slate headstones carved with names like Lloyd,

At Capel Bangor, once, there were scales and a chocolate machine.

Williams, Hughes, Thomas and Pugh. Sheep had rubbed against the barbed wire fences and left little twists of wool behind. Mr Davies gave a sharp toot on his whistle and I hastened back, noting that there were sweet violets and thrift, lady's smock, wood sorrel and forget-me-nots in the hedgerows.

Mr Davies now had his work cut out. In the course of the next four miles we would climb no less than 48oft. The gradient is one in fifty and the bends so sharp that some are laid with double rails as a safety measure. Far below us was the Cwm Rheidol reservoir and the fish ladder which enables salmon and sea trout to ascend to the head of the valley and spawn in the dangerous, sunless waters celebrated by Wordsworth in 'The Torrent at Devil's Bridge'. The Rheidol Stag came next, a huge, deer-shaped scar made in the forests on the north flank of the valley by the dumping of toxic wastes from a local lead mine. The area was once pitted with mines, and it was to carry the lead and zinc down to Aberystwyth that the line was built at the turn of the century. The earliest engines hauled little four-plank wagons laden with ore but, since the mines

Edwardian bank holiday crowds spill from the train at Devil's Bridge.

~ ARRIVAL. AT DEVIL'S BRIDGE. ~

happened to be located along one of the loveliest valleys in the British Isles, there was soon a demand from trippers for transport up to the beauty spots; the miners wanted accommodation on the train too, so that they and their families could get into town on market day. The first passenger coaches, built of red deal and pitchpine, were ordered. With the approach of World War 1, the army established camps along the line and more carriages were needed to ferry the soldiers and their stores up to the emergency military halts. At the same time the company began laying on Specials. Many were booked for the revivalist meetings held in the valley, the congregations gathering in makeshift canvas pavilions equipped with harmoniums and portable pulpits. The Rev Gypsy Smith was especially favoured by the Vale of Rheidol directors because his fire-and-brimstone rhetoric sold more seats than a cheap weekend excursion to London.

The Rheidol Falls, from this height, were just a bit of froth on an otherwise placid stream. This had been the heart of the mining country. Here you had the Gwaith Coch mine and, over the river, the massive Cwm Rheidol which sent its ore over for loading at Rhiwfron Halt by aerial ropeway; further old diggings lay ahead, up around Devil's Bridge. The line ran along a narrow rocky shelf and I noted, beneath our wheels, a sheer six-hundred-foot drop to the valley floor below. It was no place for people troubled by heights and I recalled that a visiting railway official was stricken with such severe vertigo during his first trip that, at the top, he got off and refused to get back on again, saying that he would prefer to walk home, *despite being inconvenienced by a wooden leg*. And a local mine manager always travelled with his face turned to the rock wall; if the poor man inadvertently peeped the wrong way he instantly vomited over the edge.

A row of empty fire buckets at the Devil's Bridge station.

112

The views, not surprisingly, were stupendous, the slopes bursting with greenery; feathery young spruces planted along the line kept reaching out and brushing the carriages. An RAF Tornado jet on a training run went shrieking past below, and I wondered what the pilot thought when he saw, high above, a small tank engine coming at him out of the sun. At the head of the valley we chugged through a rocky cutting and there, before us, was the end of the line. In a clearing stood the chocolate and cream station house, a homely structure with an airy veranda and a row of empty fire buckets hanging from an outside wall. Mr Davies, face furrowed and shiny with sweat, banged his regulator shut and applied the brakes. When everyone had disembarked and hurried off to the beauty spots, he disconnected the *Owain Glyndwr* and ran it around to connect with the other end of the train; later in the afternoon he would work it back down to Aberystwyth, tender first. Then he went off to the tiny buffet where he sat down, placed his cap on the table and swallowed several cups of tea.

Through the land of Tweed and Corn

NORWICH TO SHERINGHAM

Norwich is said to have thirty-two medieval parish churches within its boundaries – and that doesn't include the cathedral or the deconsecrated properties sold off and turned into theatres, health studios or garden centres. A further sixteen stand along the 30½-mile track leading north past the Broads to Cromer and Sheringham. These are village churches, and the ones not visible from the train – tucked away behind trees, perhaps – are nevertheless close enough to the metals for the worshippers to hear the tuneless blare of passing whistles, and for the travellers to stay within earshot of the bells; it takes an hour to make the journey and it would be possible, in theory, to have plain courses of Gransire Triples following one all the way up.

A stretch of track undulates across the Broads.

The line to Sheringham begins at Norwich station, an airy structure of red brick and yellow stone topped by a French pavilion roof. I followed it, one lovely summer's afternoon, in the company of a driver named Reg Reynolds. A large, slow-speaking, friendly man, he was born beside the line – his father was a local farm worker – and has since spent forty-two very good years trundling around it and the rest of East Anglia's rural network. His train, a ramshackle little two-carriage DMU powered by antique engines, left on time, launching itself out upon the broad tracery of metals that spans the approach to Norwich. But, almost at once, we slewed across to one side, away from the glittering mainline rails and on to a lacklustre, slightly rusty track that took us past Wensum Junction and along the reedy River Yare. Mr Reynolds drew my attention to a signal. 'See?' he said. 'He's giving me a caution because I'm going on the branch. At Whitlingham Junction the Sheringham metals go one way, the Yarmouth and Lowestoft ones the other.'

The Whitlingham box, designed like a miniature alpine chalet, was badly in need of a lick of paint. We began ascending our first hill, diesels labouring. 'Gradients is what this line is known for,' Mr Reynolds remarked. 'People don't usually associate the Broads with gradients, but we've got them, all right – long, gradual hauls like this one, switchbacks, really, up one side, down the other. In the steam days here on the Cromer road the old V One tanks were the best locos for heavy gradients. You needed your sand open, though, specially on a thick morning when the mist was blowing off the water.'

I said I thought the line was known for medieval churches, and Mr Reynolds agreed that this was also true. 'I would say it was *best* known for gradients, though,' he said. 'Oh, and for gates. We've got at least thirty gates and thirty crossings along here but, of course, there are churches too, I won't deny it.'

We were passing through plantations of young pines, fields of wheat and long summer grass, the track's endless rising and falling giving us the motion of a ship riding a long mid-ocean swell on a windless day. Mr Reynolds announced that we were approaching Salhouse. The church there has a fifteenth-century tower, an hour glass fixed to the pulpit and a tiny, ancient sanctus bell, while the station consists of two wooden pavilions – still with their Great Eastern canopies – standing eccentrically in the middle of a field. A girl waited on the Up platform, but she seemed anxious and absorbed and hardly noticed us as we came creaking to a halt. She was very thin and tanned and on her brown, bony wrist she wore an incongruous watch – one of those massive Seikos that can tell the time in three world capitals a hundred fathoms under water. Nobody got on our train and nobody got off. The girl continued to look worried and we pulled out again, passing a field where the wheat seemed to be sprouting through concrete.

During World War II there had been more than eighty airfields in East Anglia, and Mr Reynolds confirmed that this had been one of them. 'Just over there, beyond the fence, was where they parked "F for Freddie",' he said. 'The crew always waved when we steamed past. I remember those young chaps in their sheepskin jackets smiling and waving. After each mission they painted a

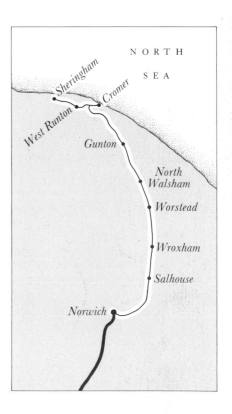

Driver Reg Reynolds.

white bomb on the nose of the plane, and we used to count those bombs and wonder how long their luck would last. Well, it lasted up to the seventeenth white bomb and after that we never saw them again. The place where "F for Freddie" stood was left empty for a few days, with just streaks of her oil on the concrete, and then another plane was put there. We used to carry a lot of flyers, of course. There was one particular train they used, the Late Night Troop Special that left Norwich for Cromer at 23.15 on Saturday nights, after the Hippodrome had closed.'

We were moving along quite smartly now, past woods and copses and tall, impenetrable hedgerows that gave the fields they surrounded the shadowy intimacy of bedrooms. Arthur Ransome wrote about this section of the line in his novel *Coot Club*. 'The train was slowing up. It crossed another river, and for a moment they caught a glimpse of moored houseboats with smoke from their chimneys where people were cooking midday meals, an old mill, and a bridge, and a lot of masts behind it. And then the train had come to a stop at Wroxham station.' That was the Wroxham approach in 1934 and, though the old mill has gone, the description remains accurate. Somnolent families sunned themselves on the decks of their motor cruisers, their pale English skins turning the colour of corned beef, their soft, plump bodies moist and slack in the heat. From the station I looked down on the premises of R. Moore and Son, Small Boat Division, and then along the line at a large warehouse which Mr Reynolds said was full of artificial manure. 'It used to be used for storing brewer's and distiller's grains,' he said. 'Tons and tons of the stuff was shipped out of here by train, most of it to Scotland. There was a time when you could *smell* the barley along this line.'

We pulled out of Wroxham. On either side of us the sugar beet fields were scalloped like sections of choppy green sea, the ripening wheat as lustrous and richly textured as brocade. The train ambled past Two Saints Farm and Belaugh Green and a succession of churches. There was St Swithin's, Ashmanhaugh, which contains the tomb of Honor Bacon, who died suddenly on the morning of her wedding day, and St Mary's, Tunstead, set in trees and boasting a rood screen painted in 1470, and St Bartholomew's, Sloley, which has a thirteenth-century chancel and a fine font. The Sloley church stands so close to the line that in the evening the train almost clips its shadow. 'The old chap up at Sloley Hall passed on yesterday,' said Mr Reynolds. 'They're burying him in that churchyard on Monday, I hear. He was eighty-eight and a bit of a character.'

The train waddled along the undulating track, its odd rocking motion making everyone sway from side to side like a revivalist congregation earnestly praising the Lord. Worstead, a centre of Norfolk's booming medieval woollen industry, lay dead ahead; it was the local weaving tycoons, keen to flaunt their money and status, who had filled the county with churches. The actual source of their wealth was the Norfolk sheep, now extinct, which had a pointed chin and long mottled legs and a fleece that, though susceptible to complaints like bloom dip, was remarkably robust. Defoe, visiting Norwich in 1723, noted that

118

on weekdays the streets were empty because the people were all indoors toiling at their looms. Worstead's church, set in the middle of the village a clear mile from its station, is a grandiose fourteenth-century structure the size of a small cathedral. Appropriately, the St Mary's Guild of Weavers, Spinners and Dyers still meets regularly to work the fourteen looms tucked away behind the elegant carved oak box pews.

The village, of course, has given its name to the English language. Worsted cloth, spun from long-staple wool, was invented by the itinerant Flemish weavers who settled in the village during the reign of Henry I. Yorkshire mills still produce over a hundred million square yards of the stuff each year, most of it going to America where it remains a fabric much favoured by members of the East Coast Establishment. You see a lot of worsted around Washington, Wall Street and the Ivy League universities but, paradoxically, one place you don't see any worsted at all is in Worstead itself. An informal survey conducted by myself in its sleepy, sun-dappled lanes several days afterwards, revealed a marked preference for denim, Indian cotton and man-made fibres. A pensioner buying apples and cream at the village shop told me that his jacket had been made in Hong Kong. 'But I wouldn't know from what,' he said. 'Certainly nothing that came off the back of a sheep.'

There was a solitary man standing on the Worstead platform. He said that the station-master's house, built of mellow red brick and set in a cool, shady garden, was now privately owned. As we moved out Mr Reynolds remarked; 'That was the level-crossing keeper, that chap. He's a good old boy, a redundant plate layer till he got them gates. See that fence over there? Used to be lined with pear trees. That was Westwick Fruit Farm land. It was all canned here, the fruit, loaded into wagons and shipped off by rail all over the place. This is good fruit country, Worstead. It's good corn country, too, and your potatoes and sugar beet also do very well.'

A few miles further on there had been a violent local storm and the fields of battered, rotting wheat were starting to smell musty. Beyond, in a stand of trees, stood the Westwick obelisk, a tall stone tower from which a jealous woman had once kept an eye on the comings and goings of her husband. Set in the trees was St Botolph's church, while another was visible on a low hill far away on the horizon – St Peter and St Paul at Honing, Mr Reynolds thought. We pressed on through fields of purple flowers and past Lord Anson's Wood and then coasted to a halt in North Walsham's big, echoing station, where there was a bit of a wait. 'Once you found coal merchants at every stop along this line,' Mr Reynolds said. 'Some stations had two. North Walsham had *four*, and every nugget came by train. North Walsham also had its own Parcels Office, employing thirty men, and it was the Parcels that shipped in the agricultural implements for the villages all around; I once drove a train carrying no fewer than *six ploughs*. Outward traffic was mostly Smedleys, of course, their tinned beans, peas, strawberries and so on. For the sugar beet they laid on Specials in season.'

Across the road from the station were the playing fields of Paston Grammar

School, which Nelson attended from 1768 to 1771. Boys were practising at the nets, though without much enthusiasm; one batted with an ice lolly stuck in his mouth. 'Mushrooms grow in the hedge over there,' said Mr Reynolds. 'When I was a lad, just joined the railways, first thing in the morning we'd sneak across and, if the early porters hadn't got there before us, we'd pick 'em and have 'em for tea.'

A rogue bank of cloud had sneaked in off the North Sea and blisters of rain suddenly spangled the windscreen. As the thunder rumbled the grammar school boys in their whites abandoned the nets and fled, whooping, for the pavilion. The drops were enormous, like marbles, and they fell torrentially. Mr

The church at Worstead, once the centre of Norfolk's booming woollen industry.

Reynolds frowned and switched on his wiper but it was ineffective, like a spoon stirring soup, so he switched it off. Then, abruptly, the rain ceased and, within minutes, the sun was beating down again, extracting a dense band of steam from the track before us. It waved and flapped like a curtain as we moved off through it, filling the train with damp volcanic vapours and fogging up the windows.

The 147ft tower of the North Walsham church fell over in 1724, the bells clanging wildly as they bounced away through the graveyard. A century later the stump collapsed as well and today the place looks devastated, as though blitzed by waves of Phantoms. At Antingham, further down the line, there is another ecclesiastical freak, a churchyard containing *two* churches, one in good repair, the other an ivy-clad Norman ruin. More followed. We saw a distant structure which might have been Trunch, famous for a stupendous font canopy, and others which were probably Swafield and Bradfield, the latter still illuminated by oil lamps and boasting a tiny organ in an ancient walnut case. St Andrew's, Gunton, set in the grounds of Gunton Park, is the only Norfolk church designed by Robert Adam; with its massive Tuscan columns it looks like a temple in a rich man's garden.

The sky had resumed its milky summer haze, deepening at the dome to a real South Seas blue. Running past Gallows Hill and the Gunton estate Mr Reynolds drove with his arms folded and propped on the control panel before him, as though leaning on a gate, his manner contemplative as he surveyed the passing countryside. The fields trembled slightly in the heat and the trees threw deep, strong shadows. A flight of wood pigeons scattered before us and he chuckled. 'On thick mornings you get pheasants standing up on the rails to get their feet out of the wet, and you hit them one after the other, boink, boink, boink. Down they go like ninepins, boink, boink, boink. The permanent way gangs pick them up and take them home and roast them with parsnips, lucky devils. Some weeks they've got pheasant coming out of their ears.'

He drew up at Gunton, where the station buildings on the Down platform have been sold and converted into a house. We found ourselves gazing into an elegant living room, richly carpeted and furnished. There were comfortable armchairs, polished brass table lamps and vases of massed flowers. Kindling was neatly stacked on the platform by the back door and, where a Great Eastern booking clerk had once sold tickets, a woman now stood in a scullery washing carrots. She had the undivided attention of everyone aboard our train, but rewarded our interest with an air of bored indifference. 'We'll be passing Southrepps Hall soon,' Mr Reynolds remarked as we swung leftwards out of the station. 'It was once owned by the Tyler brothers, duck specialists and rearers of rhubarb. All this is Gurney land. Once I stopped a train here and picked a tortoise off the track which belonged to Miss Gurney over there at Laurels Farm. It was walking to Norwich.'

Southrepps village has a large, imposing church. At Northrepps village there is a house called Templewood, built in 1938 as a shooting box for Sir Samuel Hoare and incorporating sphinxes on the terrace and a veranda propped up by columns pinched from the Bank of England. This was the prettiest part of the line, a surprising succession of hidden hillsides, tiny, shadowy fields bursting with ripening barley and incandescent poppies, small cottages tucked away in the woods, secret gardens full of foxgloves.

'Cromer Hall is owned by the Manners family,' said Mr Reynolds, indicating that we were approaching its environs. 'And that house down there belongs to the Beazleys.' There was a sudden tang of salt in the air and, between two bluffs, we saw a coaster trudging across a pale, oily sea, a line of dark smoke ascending vertically from its funnel like a single brush stroke. In *Emma* Jane

Austen observes, 'Perry was at Cromer once, and he holds it to be the best of all sea-bathing places'; but that was before the appearance of chalet-style executive bungalows, and an excrescence of caravans on the clifftop turf. The train passed the grassy viaduct, its rails long gone, which had once carried the London expresses west towards Sheringham. Ahead lay the three-quarter-mile line we would follow into Cromer and later, retracing our steps, travel down backwards towards our destination. Far below, in the midst of this grassy triangle, stood a spacious house in which a party was taking place; the house – when the expresses ran – was the only one in Britain entirely surrounded by railways. We slid into a deep fern-covered cutting, heading for Cromer and the highest church in Norfolk. The tower of St Peter and St Paul reaches 160ft above ground level, and the building is a particularly splendid one – though parish records show that during the Victorian era it suffered such

Queen Alexandra arrives at Cromer High station to catch a train in 1907.

Midsummer cornfields.

neglect that the churchwardens were obliged to purchase hedgehogs (at fourpence each) to rid the premises of vermin.

Mr Reynolds pointed up the slopes of the cutting as we pulled into the Cromer station yard. 'The land up there is all railwaymen's allotments,' he said. 'And over there is the Cromer Zoo, founded by Bertram Mills's lion tamer and the daughter of Coco the Clown. From the station you can hear the beasts roaring and trumpeting, and I've seen strangers quite startled by the noise, specially at feeding time. You can see them thinking. "Hang on: this can't be right, am I in England or the bleeding African jungle?"' We stopped, apparently parked in the wings of some small and eccentric provincial theatre. The station was built in the form of a stage, across which arriving passengers were obliged to walk, avoiding the slender fluted columns holding up the roof. Mr Reynolds collected his driving handle and prepared to take himself to the other end of the train. 'Once there were daily expresses coming up here from Liverpool Street,' he said. 'Some of those trains were very well known – the

Eastern Belle, for example. There was a chap here once, Percy Eastoe, who was a restaurant car superintendent. He had got hold of a spare piece of railway land where he raised ducks, pigs and chickens on the swill from the restaurant cars, collected each evening in swill bins guarded by a rough-coated dog called Dinky. Then, first thing each morning, Percy was back at the train – *to sell them his eggs*. What a system! No overheads, all pure profit. The eggs, fresh-laid, were poached at once, and that's one of the things I remember – when they were cooking breakfast in the restaurant cars just before the London service set off. You could smell the kippers, sausages, bacon and eggs for blooming miles. It was a *bootiful* smell.'

We pulled slowly out again, past a yard to which he drew my attention. 'That was where George Ward made the old Norfolk Red bricks,' he said. The country was starting to change. The grasses were thinning, the trees becoming lean and windblown. 'The big hill between us and the sea is Beeston Hump,' he said. He sounded his whistle and, from a house beside the line, a smiling woman

A crossing near Tunstead.

125

RIGHT
Cromer's old station, the High, now dismantled.

BELOW
Cromer Beach station, still operational, with the highest church in Norfolk just visible behind.

Cromer Beach Station.

suddenly waved. 'Housebound,' he explained. 'Crippled and can't get out, poor dear. All the drivers give her a toot when they pass. I'll tell you a strange thing. You see all those tents and the different colours of the fabric they are made from? Well, driving past at night when they've all got their lamps lit and burning inside is fantastic, the weirdest thing you ever saw, like a giant kaleidoscope or a night sky full of huge coloured stars.'

The train passed an angular modern church and a fireman's training tower. Sheringham's tiny halt lay ahead, the platform a brief footnote at the bottom of a row of back gardens. A plump white cat slept in the branches of a fig tree and a wooden hut nearby advertised itself as a 'Spiritualist Sanctuary'. Across the street from the end of the platform, a store called Jokers announced that it was 'The Small Shop With the Big Bargains'. I wandered down to have a look. One sign trumpeted, 'Yes! We Still Have Slime' while another announced the arrival of a new consignment of Prince Charles's ears.

I returned to the train. A woman in a violet coat told me that Lincolnshire had had four inches of rain the previous Tuesday. I asked her if there were any churches in Sheringham and she laughed and said: 'Of course there are. Haven't you heard our local joke? About the late Rev Fitch?' I shook my head and she said: 'Well, a widow dreamt that her husband had finally arrived at the Pearly Gates. He had told St Peter his name, and said that he had come from Sheringham. St Peter said, "Wot, not Sheringham, Norfolk?" and the man said, "Ah, thass roite." St Peter said, "Surely not the Rev Fitch's Sheringham?" The man said, "Ah, thass roite, thass the one," and Peter said, "Why, do you come straight in, then. We don't get many of his lot here."'

Skye boat-train

INVERNESS TO KYLE OF LOCHALSH

The 82¼-mile journey from Inverness to Kyle of Lochalsh can be divided, like a piece of music, into three distinct parts, or movements. The first, reflecting the gentle landscape of woods, meadows and cornfields through which the line starts, is elegiac and pastoral; the next, set in the towering, misty perspectives of the Highland glens, is majestic and slow; and the final one, celebrating a lovely, looping stretch of coast washed by the balmy waters of the Gulf Stream, vibrant and joyous, full of exuberance.

Of the three trains a day to Kyle, the best performance is given by the 10.40am; the other two, for much of the year, make their runs in the dark. All leave from platform seven, a corner of Inverness station so far-flung that it is probably the spot the authorities would select to park a train carrying fever victims or a mad bomber. Still, if one has first taken some nourishment at the Station Hotel, famous for the size and quality of its British Breakfasts, the forced march to the Kyle platform can be endured without too much hardship.

In the summer the 10.40 service includes an observation car built in 1930 for the directors of the Great Western. It contains a kitchen and two saloons furnished with the kind of armchairs and sofas usually found in stately homes; on payment of a small surcharge passengers may sit and listen to a running commentary given on the car's public address system by Mrs Barbara Pratt, a beautiful carriage cleaner from Lancashire who looks not unlike Veronica Lake in her prime. She has long golden hair, eyes the colour of Arctic ice, lovely bones and a very pleasant personality. During the long months of winter British Rail, inexplicably, make her swab down their rolling stock but, when the days start to lengthen and her gleaming chocolate and cream car is coupled to the back of the train again, she clears her throat, takes up her microphone and becomes, once more, the Voice of the Glens.

This is really the train to Skye – the hamlet of Lochalsh lies only a four-minute ferry ride from that massive, mysterious island – and on the August morning I chose to travel both the train and the observation car were fairly full. A comfortable, grey-haired couple sat beside me, wearing tweeds and yellow roses in their buttonholes. They lived in Inverness, they said, and made this journey every summer, taking lunch and high tea at the Lochalsh Hotel before catching the 5.10pm service home again. 'The number and nationality of our fellow passengers depends on the strength of the pound,' the man said. 'If the mark is stronger you get the Germans, if the franc is strong then it's the French.

Today we followed a party of Slavic-speaking people down the platform, so I imagine the rouble or the zloty is riding high.'

We pulled out on time and made for the nine-arch viaduct over the River Ness and, at Clachnaharry, the swing bridge spanning the Caledonian Canal. Barbara Pratt, seated at her table, pointed to the Black Isle lying across the estuary and explained that it was not an isle but an isthmus; 'black' probably derives from plundering Norsemen who had pursued a scorched earth policy. It was actually a remarkably fertile stretch of country, famous for its crops and cattle and a witch named Hairy Agnes.

We trundled through fields of grain and, near the Mains of Bunchrew, past an abandoned station with a pretty pink house and a platform grassy as a tennis lawn, its verge badly chipped. The tide was out and the estuary glassily reflected the huge Highland sky. At Muir of Ord we saw the cairn marking the spot where, a century ago, a demented Irish harpist murdered Lord Macdonald of the Isles; at Canon Bridge the lady from Inverness told me that the village used to be known for the beauty and colour of its cottage gardens. 'On a warm summer's evening the scents could take your breath away,' she said. We clattered into Dingwall where they still have a few fragments of the castle in which, it is alleged, Macbeth's father was born. The station was fashioned from lovely pale-pink Tarradale stone, quarried on the Black Isle, with elegant

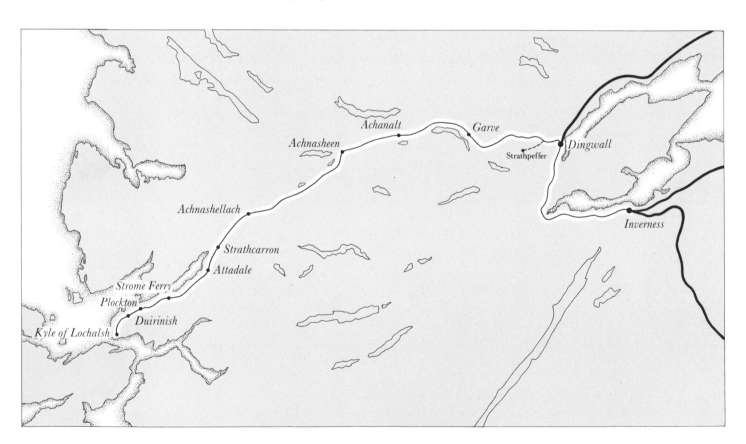

iron pillars supporting the ornate glass platform canopy. A polished brass plaque on the wall near Munro's bookstall announced that, on that spot during World War 1, no fewer than 134,864 servicemen had been given cups of tea.

I leant out of the window and spoke to a man carrying a small box. He said he worked in Parcels and when I asked him whether business was brisk he gave me a pained look. 'Are you joking?' he said. 'Parcels have all but disappeared on this line. Now we only get about a barrowload a day.' What killed off Parcels – and Freight – on the Skye run, he told me, was the Beeching edict forbidding the carriage of livestock on the railways.

'We used to get a lot of traffic from the Skye and Stornaway crofters coming down to the sales here. And the movement of wintering sheep from summer grazing in the Highlands and back again kept us very busy too. I can remember the streets outside the station here being so full of beasts you could barely move – sheep, pigs and fat cattle bound for Glasgow, the drovers and their dogs herding them down to the loading banks. One year we had 184,000 animals through Dingwall, and the Specials were going out till the early hours of the morning. We had our own loco shed, our own engines, our own drivers. We even had one chap who did nothing but wash cattle trucks. Now all the livestock is going by road and the only freight I have for this service today is one package for Plockton, perishable, fishy smell, probably a salmon.'

He went forward to leave it with the guard and, a few moments later, we pulled out and headed for the junction where the Further North Line to Wick and Thurso began its journey into latitudes boasting frosts that can snap steel rails like pretzels; we bore left, however, and ambled through ripe cornfields towards the Western Isles. 'Just over here on the slopes of Knockfarril,' Barbara Pratt was saying, 'the Mackenzies and Macdonalds fought a bloody battle. To promote good relations between the clans the son of a Mackenzie chief had married a Macdonald girl but, unfortunately, she only had one eye; and a chance argument with a Macdonald gave him the excuse he needed to get rid of his rather plain wife. He sent her home on a one-eyed horse with a one-eyed attendant and a one-eyed dog and, within hours, the clans were at war.'

Everyone smiled and, seeing that she had come to a break in her commentary, I went forward to ask how she rated her audience today. 'Oh, not bad at all,' she said. 'I can usually tell from that one-eyed Macdonald story. A good bunch of passengers will always respond; it's when they look at me blankly that I know I'm going to have my work cut out. Only once have I not been able to tell it, and that was when there was a one-eyed chap sitting right opposite me and not looking too pleased with life anyway. Not that you can always judge by appearances. I had a man once who came aboard carrying a plastic shopping bag. He never spoke a word but, near Kyle, the train was held up. It was a warm day and after we had been sitting there for twenty minutes or so he suddenly held up his shopping bag and spoke for the first time. "I've got two haggises in here," he said in a loud Lancashire voice, "and if we don't move

Mrs Barbara Pratt, observation car commentator and Voice of the Glens.

soon they're going to crawl out of this bag and get off.'' A moment later the train started and the chap never opened his mouth again.'

She turned back to her microphone to point out the site of Fodderty Junction and the grassy lane curving off to the left along which the Strathpeffer metals had once been laid. The resort, glimpsed in the distance, clambered along the sides of a steep green valley. Once it had been served by crack trains like the Strathpeffer Spa Express speeding along the Picturesque Line of the Empire and promoted by intensive advertising campaigns; the Minister Muses, for example, showed a gloomy, dyspeptic parson sitting morosely over his sermon notes and 'longing for a sight of Strathpeffer'.

My Inverness friend offered me whisky from a silver hip flask. It was a Skye malt, strong and smoky, and as I sipped it we slipped through Auchterneed station, now privately owned and set in a lawn with a mossy platform running down the middle. The engine wheezed as it began its scramble over the 458ft summit of Raven Rock. 'These old Class 26 locomotives often have trouble about here,' he said. 'In poor weather the wheels slip and, more often than not, there are mechanical problems; the engines are just about the oldest still knocking about in Scotland. There is no fitter out at Kyle, so the drivers often have to make their own running repairs. As well as that, it's a difficult line to drive – curves, gradients, short platforms, the constant threat of rock falls. All the Class 26s now carry searchlights and radios. The radios have made a big difference: in the old days if there was trouble the drivers sometimes had to hoof it for miles.'

The diesels cracked and roared as we approached the menacing pinnacle of Raven Rock. Then we descended through a forest so dense and damp it might have been tropical; along its perimeter birch leaves caught the sun and glinted like new coins. We rattled over the Blackwater, a dark, shadowy stream stealing through the trees, and along the southern shore of Loch Garve, finally slowing beside a meadow full of yellowing summer grass. Behind, pines sprouted as thick as whiskers on the slopes of Little Wyvis; above a curving treeline, the hill was bald and brightly flushed with heather. Garve is known to collectors of railway lore as a passing place for ships. The Up and Down tracks were laid ten feet apart to accommodate the fleets of gaudily painted wooden trawlers which, it was once hoped, would be loaded aboard special wagons and rushed to whichever coast was providing the best catches.

Garve station is in the charge of Alec MacKenzie, or Big Alec, a 19½-stone caber-tossing champion who told me he thought he lay about third in the Scottish merit tables. 'I certainly came third in the last World Caber-Tossing Championships at Aberdeen,' he said. 'Most weekends during the season I'm in action at Highland Games somewhere and it's difficult at any one moment to know precisely where you stand.' Not that his travels are restricted to Scotland. 'I went to Johannesburg last year to give demonstrations at the Rand Show,' he said. 'And I've been out to the old Queen Mary in California to play the accordion. That is my other interest. On the Queen I gave them a week of Scottish country dance music.'

Noting that the train was ready to move he stood back and raised a massive arm to the driver, causing a momentary eclipse of the sun. A gradient took us past a hotel, a field of cabbages and the croft in which Ramsay MacDonald's grandfather had been born. This fact, together with the observation that someone had recently painted its roof, was given to me by the ticket inspector, a large, ebullient man named Jack Rennie.

We climbed away from a bright river and, ascending Corriemollie Summit, burst through the treeline on to a huge, bare moor carpeted with heather. A waterfall came foaming out of the hillside and under the line, emptying into a rushing, turbulent river which swirled along beside the train and then began changing shape, its banks moving eccentrically this way and that until, quite unexpectedly, they sprang apart and turned into the head of a loch. We were moving fast now, rushing through a landscape full of streams and water meadows, entering Strath Bran, Valley of the Drizzle, and heading for the tiny halt at Achanalt. I joined Mr Rennie and Francis Coghill, the guard, in Mr Coghill's old steam-heated van. They had had an arduous morning, Mr Coghill being obliged to write out, in his fastidious longhand, every ticket sold aboard. Now, surrounded by swirling clouds of vapour, he sat and ate his sandwiches.

'The Marquesa de Torrehermosa lives here at Achanalt,' he said. 'Her husband, the Marquis, is buried right in front of the house with a flock of geese always standing guard near the grave.'

'The Marquesa also answers to the name of Mrs McPhee,' said Mr Rennie.

'I met her, you know,' said Mr Coghill, a dark, intense, kindly man. 'A couple of months ago the Scottish Chamber Orchestra brought a chartered steam train down this line for an outing, and the Marquesa was aboard. The musicians had turned my van into a bar and buffet. What fun everyone had! That was a truly joyful day.'

The River Bran, in spate, shared the floor of the strath with us, and it too made odd little rushes at the line. All about us were the vast perspectives of the Western Highlands: on one side a lofty mountain shaped like a headless sphinx; on the other a steep, misty slope, its covering of wet bracken and heather giving it a bruised and sombre look. We coasted slowly into Achnasheen, the line's main passing place and the spot where we would meet the 11.10am Up train from Kyle of Lochalsh. It was running late, so I was promised time to jump down and look around. Beyond the station was a scattering of small houses and, by the main road, a petrol station. The Down platform was surfaced with pinkish gravel, and a rowan tree grew beside the little iron footbridge that led across the line to one of the strangest hotels in Britain. It was built in 1870 to provide passengers with food and shelter, and designed to be part of the station. The front door opened on to the Up platform, and so did the dining room, its tables now neatly laid for lunch. The first landlord, Murdo McIver, had been a devout Presbyterian whose observance of the Sabbath was so scrupulous that, when Queen Victoria arrived by coach from Loch Maree one Sunday afternoon, he denied her fresh horses and refused to post her mail. The Queen of Earthly Queens, miffed but helpless, is alleged to have checked in, eaten a plate of cold roast beef and decided on an early night.

Keen to meet the present owner I went indoors – today the main entrance faces the road – and learnt from a brochure that the place was now 'under the

Fred Field, ex-carriage cleaner in charge of Achnasheen station.

personal supervision of Beryl and Sid Abraham'. Mr Abraham appeared a moment later. A heavy, lugubrious man, he had worked as an engineer in West Africa but always dreamt of living in the Highlands. 'A lot of our guests are train enthusiasts,' he said. 'This hotel is famous in their circles and it draws them like a magnet. Oddly enough, quite a few of them are railwaymen. We get lots of British Rail personnel coming here for their holidays. I've even spotted Sir Peter Parker drinking incognito in the lounge bar. Some people actually catch railway fever after they've arrived. There was a family who checked in late one night last year, not realising there was anything different about the place. When they were awakened next morning by a very old locomotive pulling up under their window they went quite barmy with excitement; this summer they came back and stayed a whole week.'

Earlier, outside, I had seen a man marching down the track towards the signal-box. He had a military bearing, long white hair, a flowing white beard and a peaked cap jauntily shaped and blocked so that it resembled the type worn by young U-boat commanders. I asked a lady working in the hotel who he was and she said: 'That's Captain Birdseye, alias Fred Field. He runs the station.'

I returned to the platform and, noting that the Up train had still not appeared, knocked at the door of the station office. A strong voice commanded me to enter. Mr Field sat at a desk which massively reflected the days when the station-master was a figure of weight and substance in the community. He was flanked by an ancient Bolton Chatwoods Double Patent wall-safe and a large, sonorously ticking clock made by J. G. Brown of Glasgow.

I asked him where he came from and he told me that he was Dorset-born, but had been accepted by the Seaforth Highlanders at fourteen because he had enough Scottish blood in him to satisfy the regiment's ruling on the subject. 'I was a boy soldier and although I left the army in 1948 I am still allowed to wear the Seaforth kilt. That is my privilege for life and I wore it at my wedding.' After his military service he took up psychiatric nursing but, eventually, felt obliged to give it up. 'My superior started behaving violently towards a patient of mine who had become incontinent so I quit in disgust and, at Inverness, became a carriage cleaner. I suppose, in railway terms, that carriage cleaning is just about the lowest form of life, but the industry is full of old cleaners like me who have gone on to better things. I love it here. One of the best times is Sundays, when there are no trains running. Around mid-morning the deer begin coming down to the station, twenty, thirty, forty of them cautiously descending the hillside to crop the grass along the rails.'

The train from Kyle was approaching and he stuck on his cap and hurried off to attend to it. I noted a sign telling the drivers to change radio channels and, nearby, the remains of a stone water column in which, once, a fire had burnt throughout the winter to stop the contents freezing. I returned to the train and told Mr Coghill I thought Achnasheen was a bit of a dump. 'Och, I don't know,' he said. 'At least the climate's healthy. I knew a signalman from here who got married at sixty and fathered a wee boy.'

Achnasheen, where the trains pass and the hotel dining room opens on to the platform.

135

We crossed a bustling, frothy stream and laboured up an incline past a few solitary houses and another hotel, fashioned from pink stone and set in a grove of trees. The moor hereabouts was nondescript, though I noted a hillside planted with strange, stunted trees, like a grove of blighted olives. The waters of Loch Gowan looked dark and cold and deep. Luib Summit, at the top of the line, was a marshy wilderness, a desolation of hummocks tricked out in scraggy heather and tussocks of yellowing grass. There were a couple of surfacemen's cottages nearby, weather-beaten little dwellings for the gangs tending the permanent way. They stand close to the Drumalbain watershed, the precise point high on the spine of Scotland where the pull of the seas on either side divides the streams, sending some flowing down to the east, others to the west.

We began descending through mist. Up here the air was chill, with a sharp, autumnal edge to it, but the clouds of warm steam billowing benignly through the guard's van kept the atmosphere temperate. We picked up speed, rattling down the old line to the banks of Loch Scaven with its tiny wooded islands; plumb in the middle of the lake a solitary fisherman stood motionless in a dinghy. 'He'll be after trout, salmon or pike,' observed Mr Coghill. 'These sweet-water lochs are full of them.'

The high, bare hills were scattered with boulders and scree but, almost imperceptibly, the landscape was beginning to soften. The massive proportions of the high moors grew more human and manageable, the washed-out colours of stone and scrub giving way to robust greens and purples; a stray sunbeam glanced off a rockface and made it sparkle. Above us an elegant grey house clung to the side of a steep valley. 'That's Glencarron Lodge,' said Mr Rennie, 'the home of Lady Cobbold, an eccentric Victorian traveller said to have been the first white woman to have got into Mecca. She adopted the Muslim faith and is buried there in her garden, standing up and facing east. The railway used to deliver her milk.'

Her halt, a private stop, once had a set of semaphore signals on the platform; anyone wanting to catch the train operated them himself, throwing the levers when he heard the old Skye Bogie puffing up the glen. The valley floor below was carpeted with spiky Scots pines, but in Achnashellach Forest, reached moments later, the spruces, alders, willows, birches, hollies and oaks grew with a kind of equatorial lustre. The station stood in a clearing. It was an enchanted spot, hidden deep in the woods with a massive shoulder of rock, mossy and cloud-capped, rearing high overhead. 'Achnashellach,' said Mr Coghill, 'means Field of the Willows. This was a private station too, originally built for a Mr Tennant. The Dingwall and Skye management were too mean to give the station-master proper quarters so he had to sleep in his office, a wooden platform shack that only cost them fifty quid. One night in 1892 there was a very odd accident here, when an evening Mixed became separated from its engine and rolled away down the steep gradient below the halt. The footplate crew, when they had got over their shock, set off after it. But they had forgotten that at the bottom of the hill the line starts to rise again. This slope had stopped the train, which was rolling back down it when it ran into its own engine, climbing hard in pursuit. A few of the passengers were bruised but, remarkably, no serious injuries were suffered.'

We slowed for a level crossing. Beside a tiny cottage a slim young man waited with a green flag. 'That is the best-educated crossing keeper in Scotland,' said Mr Rennie, and I was to have that confirmed a couple of days later when I called at the cottage and introduced myself to Peter Roy, an English biochemist and Bachelor of Science who has manned the gates for twelve years. He applied for the job because he liked the solitude and because it gave him time to make the attractive inlaid wooden boxes (two of which are owned by the Queen) that are his main interest in life.

His duties on the railway are not onerous. Six times a day he must open the gates and wave the drivers through. 'If I forget them they have to stop and toot their whistles until I turn up, but they can be forgetful too. Twice during my time here the driver has gone whizzing straight through the gates, travelling fast with his mind on other things. Those gates are made of good quality pine and not a splinter was wasted. I collected all the remains and used them for furniture and toys. My bed is built from the wreckage of the first gate, and part of the second has been turned into a model sailing boat; the rest may become a Welsh dresser.'

Mr Roy, married with two small children, says it's an idyllic existence, but one which could be terminated at any moment by the closure of the line. 'They've already given me one nasty shock,' he said, 'when they threatened me a year ago with automatic barriers. That particular nightmare was avoided thanks to the local sheep, which use my crossing each morning to come down from the hill to pasture. Inverness considered the problem for some time and eventually came up with the notion of a special sheep's underpass. But the cost of automatic gates *and* an underpass would have been equivalent to my wages for the rest of my life, so they shelved the idea.'

His cottage looks out over a meandering little loch. We passed it now, on the final leg of the run to Kyle. The country was becoming flatter, some of it fenced and planted with barley. We saw a group of rounded little hills covered with ridged yellow turf, like wrinkles on an assembly of furrowed brows. The Strathcarron signal-box, approached through fields, stood in a small copse. On the wall of the station house there were climbing roses and a clock without hands. A line of pines shaded the Down platform and several wooden boxes were ranged along its length to help short-legged passengers alight. In the station yard stood a small hotel and a telephone box with its paint faded to a delicate shell pink.

'There used to be a station-master here with a parrot which could do a perfect imitation of a guard's whistle,' said Mr Rennie. 'That bird caused a bit of havoc in its time, I can tell you. When you got the guard blowing his own whistle to countermand the parrot, and the parrot whistling even louder to countermand the guard, it could sound as if there was a police raid in progress.'

This country was neat and tamed. Moments later blue water appeared suddenly beyond the corn and pasture. We had arrived at Loch Carron and the

Peter Roy, a qualified biochemist, is 'the best-educated crossing keeper in Scotland'.

Evening train near Kyle.

sea. The sun slid out from behind a black cloud and caught a small white church on the far shore, making its windows flash. We passed a football field with a piebald horse grazing in a goalmouth and then a pair of cottages beside a cutting, going so close that I could have reached out and swiped an onion from a kitchen windowsill. The track slid under a massive concrete avalanche shelter and then took us on down the loch, the rising tide almost foaming under the wheels. A seal emerged from the sea a few feet away and gave us a bored, indifferent look. It was chewing something, possibly a salmon, and water dripped from its bushy whiskers.

There was a brief stop at Attadale, built in 1873 as a private halt for the local MP. 'It's still private, though now it's Mr McPherson's stop, this one,' Mr Coghill said. 'Of course, the public are entitled to use it too. Glencarron is private also. We only stop there for the Lodge.'

Winter on the Kyle line early in the century.

142

Stromeferry station house is a curious, barnlike structure the colour of mustard. Piles of rusting iron pipes lay about the station yard, the property of Howard Doris, the consortium which builds oil rigs at Loch Kishorn nearby. The Strome ferry service was discontinued several years ago, but the concrete landing where the cars went ashore on the other side is still visible. This was the line's original terminus, and its completion in 1870 was celebrated by a gala dinner on the platform of the new station. Whisky, claret and port were served, and the pipers brought in from Dingwall got so smashed that 'they could neither blow, stand up nor all play the same tune'. A pier was built at Strome, and little railway steamers like the *Carham*, propelled by paddlewheels and a double steeple engine, and the *Ferret*, later highjacked to Australia, plied between Strome and Portree on Skye. And, at the insistence of the Northern Lights Commissioners, the company placed beacons and marker buoys around the Loch Carron approaches to make them safe for navigation.

Pulling out of Stromeferry the train passes a stone cottage and a sturdy stone bridge set at the end of the platform. I wandered back to the buffet car and, while eating an apple pie, fell into conversation with an elderly man in a neat grey suit who said he had once worked in the Kyle ticket office. 'That was back in the days when the Stornaway kipper boat came daily to Kyle and all the cargoes were sent up this line, ten or twelve wagons of Stornaway kippers worked each morning to Dingwall or Inverness. On their return they carried, for the kippering, several tons of oak chips which were then shipped back to Stornaway. Is that apple pie any good?'

'It's all right,' I said.

'Then I'll try one myself,' he said, rising and going to the counter. After he had tasted it he continued: 'The station-master I worked for was a Glaswegian who would stand no nonsense from anybody. I recall one stormy evening the door was thrown open and there, larger than life, stood Macdonald of Macdonald – the Lord of the Isles! He was just over from Skye and demanded truculently that our eight ferrymen be sacked on the grounds that the boat had run twenty minutes late because they had all been rendered incapable by drink. The station-master said the offenders would be dismissed instantly and asked when Macdonald's eight sober replacements would be arriving. Macdonald said he had no replacements, sober or otherwise. The station-master said: "Then you'll be making your own arrangements to cross the water home again, I assume? No ferrymen, no ferry, of course" – and the Lord of the Isles, glowering, withdrew his complaint and agreed that the eight offenders should be retained.'

I made my way back to the observation car. The sun was shining as we passed two pretty teenage girls standing in a field of buttercups. They were holding up large placards. One said, 'Have a good trip' and the other, 'The Kyle Line Rules OK'. Barbara Pratt gave a bemused shrug and told me that this section of the line, completed in 1897, had proved to be the costliest stretch of railway then built in Britain. It took four years to blast thirty-three cuttings out of the gneiss and quartzite, while at Kyle of Lochalsh nearly 106,000 cubic

The train passes near Duncraig Castle, once the home of the Duchess of Sutherland and now a domestic science college.

143

yards of rock were dug up to bring the station site down to sea level. Then, beside it, they built a pair of massive piers which could handle passenger and cargo ships whatever the state of the tide. 'Over there, on your right, are the peaks of Applecross,' she said, 'while the castle we are approaching is Duncraig, built by Sir Alexander Matheson, one of the founders of this line. It later became the home of the Duchess of Somerset and is now a domestic science college.'

The Duncraig halt, and the stretch of coast on which it sits, has the ordered elegance of a Japanese garden. There are groves of rhododendrons and ancient firs growing on outcrops of smooth, pale rock. Some of the cuttings are joined by mossy stone bridges leading from one shadowy wood to another and carpeted with pine needles. Small islands stand offshore, also planted with firs and looking as though they belong in a formal Oriental lake. I remarked on them to Barbara Pratt who said: 'That one over there is called the Island of the Cat, and it's owned by Dr McLaine Watt of Glasgow Cathedral.'

Plockton, perhaps the prettiest village on the line, is warmed by the Gulf Stream and has palm trees growing in its gardens. Artists winter there, yachtsmen and holidaymakers crowd it in the summer. Its grey-painted timber station has fancy bargeboards, ecclesiastical windows and yet another handless clock. The line runs on, past the Tingle Creek guest house and tin-roofed sheds stacked with peat. The water in the bays outside Kyle is real Blue Lagoon water, lying over white sand and so translucent that, for a moment or two, the shadow of our observation car ducked down and ran along the sea bed.

The Duncraig halt.

The train approaches Kyle of Lochalsh through a red rock cutting. Tucked inside the throat of the station yard is the site of the engine shed where locomotives like the Clan Goods – once the mainstay of the line – the small Bens and the McIntosh Tanks were put at night; the old Highland brake vans with their dovecot windows would have been parked out in the sidings. Until the advent of war, when the trains were laden precariously with mines, life was peaceful; in 1936, for example, the only thing to disturb the tranquillity of the line was the introduction of Stroudleys Improved Engine Green, a controversial colour regarded in some circles as quite unsuitable for the Highland locomotives.

Thirty-three cuttings were blasted from the rock on the final leg of the line, making it the most expensive stretch of railway in Britain.

A Macbrayne's paddle steamer berthed at
the Kyle station pier. The Skye ferry,
with sail (on the left), was then propelled
by the wind.

Kyle station is a graceful, single-storied building with the dimensions of a
comfortable tropical club; on the platform there were pots of heather and a
wheelbarrow full of marigolds. The train rumbled across the points and halted
in the shadow of the island. There had been heavy rain the previous day and,
scattered across the steep, bracken-coloured hills, were countless commas of
turbulent white water. The Lochalsh Hotel, just a few paces from the station,
and hard beside the Macbrayne's ferry slipway, occupies one of the world's
prime positions, standing so close to Skye that the building is filled with the
wonderful lemony stained-glass light that radiates from the island whenever
there is a break in the cloud.

I saw my Inverness friends lunching in the restaurant. They raised their
glasses, smilingly drawing my attention to the stupendous view, and it seemed
entirely appropriate that they should be toasting it in champagne.

OPPOSITE
The early morning service, equipped with
steam-heated carriages, prepares to leave
from Kyle station with Skye rearing
majestically over the water.

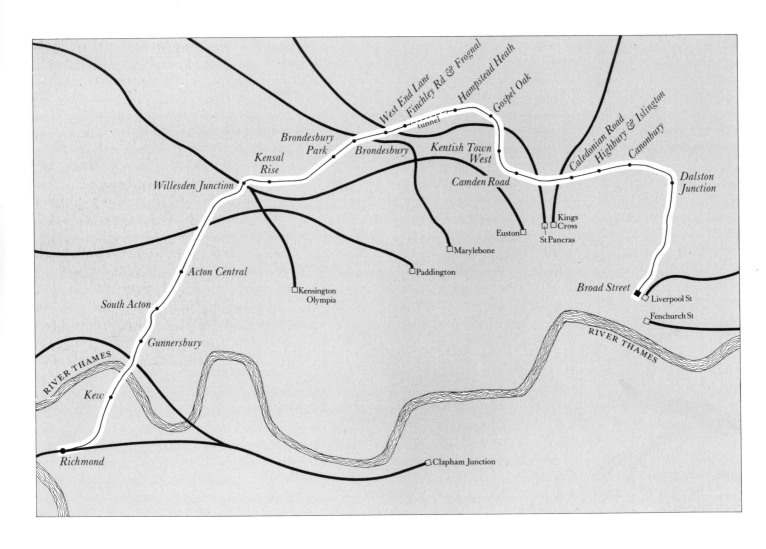

London's own rural railway

BROAD STREET TO RICHMOND

The Broad Street line goes ambling for sixteen and a quarter miles through the back gardens of London. Three times an hour the service sets out from the heart of the City and, moving at the leisurely pace of a country train, trundles south through the suburbs to the pretty riverside town of Richmond-upon-Thames. The line's relationship with the capital is a peculiarly intimate one. For much of its length it passes the backs of London's houses and shares in the domestic lives of the people who live in them. Its little trains, visible from countless kitchens, bedrooms and nurseries, are often the first – as infants – they ever see and also, sometimes, the last; one sultry summer night near Gospel Oak, for example, I glimpsed through a lit, uncurtained window two men and a red-haired priest sitting by the bed of an old woman who was clearly close to death. The line even helps feed its dependents. Here and there along its length vegetable plots have been established beside the rails; peas, runner beans, lettuces, spring onions and leeks invariably do well along the Broad Street permanent way. There are hundreds of orthodox gardens as well and, on autumnal Saturday afternoons, smoke from the burning leaves drifts into the carriages, making the passengers cough and splutter and complain of watering eyes.

Broad Street station is a rum place, an echoing, vulgar, mock-Venetian palace built on land which yielded so many human remains that it is thought to be the site of a plague pit, or perhaps the burial ground of the old Bethlehem Hospital. The *Illustrated London News*, reporting on its gala opening in 1865 – attended by the Lord Mayor and Sheriffs of London – noted tactfully that the gleaming white Suffolk brick edifice with its terracotta medallions and columns of Peterhead granite was 'rather more decorated than most stations'. There were eleven hundred windows, all of which broke in 1915 when a cruising Zeppelin dropped bombs; the baroque stained glass advertisements broke too, though the enamel Pears Soap plaques embedded in the sides of the platforms were left unscathed.

At the turn of the century there were more arrivals at Broad Street than at Euston and Paddington combined. Each weekday 794 trains deposited eighty-five thousand passengers at its seven platforms. Broad Street then served a whole array of destinations; its celebrated Wolverhampton and Birmingham 'City to City' service, for example, was worked by a luxurious businessman's express with a legion of lady typists available aboard to do letters for a small fee. It was withdrawn in 1915, some years after the station had begun to go into its

The rotting structure of Broad Street's baroque station nestles in the shadow of the City of London's soaring towers.

decline. That process started with the introduction of the electric tram, and it has continued so remorselessly down the years that Broad Street now is just an echoing, semi-derelict shadow of its former self, catering for a mere four thousand passengers a day, reconciled to the prospect of closure.

On the warm autumn afternoon that I went there for a ride down the line I noted that, at the foot of the grand central staircase – now soiled and unswept – there was a small porno shop. Upstairs on the main concourse, by contrast, stood a memorial to the North London men who fell in the Great War and, just beyond it, an abandoned shed that had once been the Guards and Shunters

A bustling Broad Street in its heyday.

Mess Room. The one remaining signal-box is perched loftily at the end of a platform set with a weathered plaque saying, 'Sixty One Feet Eight Inches South East From This Stone Is The Boundary Of The Parish Of St. Leonard Shoreditch' and signed by the church wardens who held office in 1866.

'The last steam engines into Broad Street,' said the signalman, an affable Biafran named Cosmos Ohanekwu, 'were the old Tring Residentials, used mainly at peak periods.'

Mr Ohanekwu regards his job as a logical extension of his lifelong interest in trains. 'Even as a very small boy I was collecting the numbers of the Nigerian one-liners, steam locomotives built mostly at Crewe.' As I examined a giant cogged wheel used for tightening signal wires made slack by midsummer heat, he ticked off on his fingers the boxes that had been closed on the Broad Street line. 'There is, let us see, Broad Street Number One, Skinner Street Junction, New Inn Yard, Dunloe Street, Dalston Station Junction and Canonbury station,' he said. 'Canonbury Junction, Highbury, Barnsbury, St Pancras Junction and Maiden Lane Junction. Kentish Town West, Gospel Oak Number Two, Hampstead Heath, Finchley Road, Brondesbury and Kensal Rise. Old Oak Junction, South Acton Junction and Gunnersbury. And, of course, Kew Gardens.'

I said goodbye to Mr Ohanekwu and wandered over to a far platform where the abandoned trackbed was full of buddleia and sallow and stands of small birches. A couple of summers earlier, a botanist studying the flora and fauna along these few yards of deserted railway had filled several notebooks with his findings. I clambered up a wall and saw that Liverpool Street station lay directly below me, at the foot of a precipitous drop. Jumping down again, I caused a pair of passing red admirals to rock visibly in my slipstream. The fluted call of a blackbird indicated that there were nests among the birches and buddleia. The sun was warm, the noises of the city far away. Not even the arrival of a train at platform four could disturb the tranquillity. I strolled back to the supervisor's office and met Len Armitage, a sprightly driver with a trim, nautical beard. 'I've just finished my fourth Richmond,' he said. 'That's what we aim for, four Richmonds a day if everything goes according to schedule.'

I asked him what the Richmond run was like. 'A few significant gradients,' he said, judiciously. 'From Broad Street you drop downhill to Dalston Junction. You climb back up to the Caledonian Road, level off at Camden, climb past Kentish Town and Gospel Oak, climb again to Hampstead Heath. Then it's up and down to Acton Wells and, after that, a fairly steady descent to the river and Richmond. In the old days we liked to coast down the descending gradients with our steam shut off; North London drivers were famous for their low fuel consumption and people said they put economy before punctuality; whatever the truth of the matter, those gradients helped them save coal. It's a pleasant little line to drive, and I suppose the most exciting thing that happened to me was Boxing Night 1970 when a drunk slipped down between the train and the platform as we were pulling out of Caledonian Road. He was a negro, a *huge* feller, and when we hauled him clear we found he had lost a leg. We put him in an empty carriage – unit 61144 it was; I'll always remember that number – which was brand new, fresh out of Wolverton and clean as a new pin until he bled all over it. When the ambulance took him away the railway police said, first chance they got, they were going to march him into court, wooden leg and all, and prosecute him under Section Six of the Act for travelling without a ticket.'

Mr Armitage, who joined the railways in 1937 as a Willesden tank lad, chuckled and lit a giant pipe. 'The chap you should have met was Davy Moore, used to be a supervisor here, a real character and highly artistic, kept a big box of coloured chalks for writing up announcements on the blackboard outside. Them announcements was just beautiful, genuine works of art, real . . . posters! His St George's Day ones were famous. He would write things like "By George!" on them, plays on words really, but done in beautiful lettering with scrolls and decorations and everything. He did one every St George's Day, and every St David's and St Andrew's and St Patrick's Day as well. And any other days that took his fancy. I mean, on the day the Great Northern stopped running to Broad Street he did a special poster for all their passengers saying thank you, goodbye and good luck. He gave this place a *personal* touch.'

It was time to catch my train. I said goodbye to Mr Armitage and entered an elderly carriage, noting that the platform clock, hanging beside an advertisement saying 'Time Is Money', had stopped at 2.23. Just before we pulled out a middle-aged man stepped carefully aboard. He wore a well-cut grey pinstriped suit, handmade shoes, a cream-coloured silk shirt and a Brigade of Guards tie, and he carried an uncorked bottle of hock in one hand and, in the other, a wine glass with a single gardenia stuck in it. He sat down, filled the glass and, as the train moved off past the buddleia grove, drank deeply, holding the gardenia clear with a finger. His face was full of pleasure. My fellow passengers and I smiled at him, but he neither noticed nor responded.

We ran along a tall embankment, the dowdy houses, shops and small factories of Bishopsgate stretching away on either side, the glittering towers of the City rising up behind like the battlements of some fabulous medieval fortress. That, clearly, was where our companion had come from, the bottle having been swiped from some ritzy directors' dining room; now, savouring its contents, he paid little heed to the lesser businesses we were passing – the Fancy Box and Pad Manufacturers, Gordon Fabrics, the Doughty Shoe Factors, the East London Knowledge School and the premises of a Greek who manufactured buttons.

Dalston Junction was situated at the foot of an incline and beyond an abandoned signal-box. We left the station through a long tunnel and a deep cutting from which we looked up at streets of terraced houses, the fronts of one row merging into the backs of the next. At Canonbury the drinker stood and, clutching his bottle and glass and crooning to himself, left the train. His place was taken by a youth with lank hair, vivid eczema scars and a denim jacket covered with the tiny locomotive badges that denoted a serious interest in railway matters.

Gospel Oak's pavilion-like signal box.

Canonbury station had wooden banisters ascending to street level and a cluster of bright autumnal trees growing on a slope behind a retaining greystone wall. I saw the first of the graffiti for which the line is renowned, an anti-nuclear skull and crossbones bearing the legend 'It Will Cost The Earth'. As we slid off towards Highbury and Islington the youth, seeing me scribbling in my notebook, asked me if I was a train enthusiast. I explained that I was a mere journalist recording my journey, and he told me that I had made a very good choice of route. This was an interesting line. Did I know, for example, that it had once built its own locomotives? 'At the Bow Works,' he said, 'opened by the North London directors in 1863 and covering thirty-one acres. They recruited William Adams, their first Locomotive Superintendent, from the Royal Sardinian Navy. His engines had open cabs and green livery and polished brass domes, and the carriages were varnished teak. The third class ones had no partitions, and buskers used to come aboard and entertain the passengers. That was one of the well-known things about the North London, the way you could be entertained while you travelled; I've heard it said that Paganini, for a joke, once played his violin between Barnsbury and Kentish Town with a monkey and a tin cup.'

Islington and Highbury's palatial station in 1873.

Highbury and Islington was approached through a tunnel. The words 'Killer Kate' were painted on the lofty walls rising above the platform. The run to Caledonian Road and Barnsbury was made along a cutting lined with mossy bricks. 'Walking Wounded' said the graffito on the station shelter. On the next lap, to Camden Road, a glance back the way we had come revealed stupendous views of London, the St Paul's dome massive and faintly luminous against the pale afternoon sky. Now, below us, there were suddenly railways everywhere, swathes of track ducking in and out of tunnels and going in all directions; some were headed, the young man said, for the King's Cross Freight Terminal. There was a hell of a lot of freight on the Broad Street, he told me and, even as he spoke, a huge diesel growled past hauling clanking flatcars stacked with new Fiestas. 'George Davis Is Innocent OK' said the words on a warehouse wall and then, having passed the Ebonite tower and crossed the blue iron bridge into Camden Road I saw the inevitable conclusion to that premise, weathered white capitals demanding that George Davis be freed. The station boasted four platforms and the kind of buildings, generously proportioned with vaguely ecclesiastical windows, that one would find at the station of a prosperous market town.

'The thing about this line is the number of stops,' my friend remarked. 'In 1900 the trains averaged seven thousand stops a day on the North London. The first brakes they had was the Miles steam brake. That was followed by Jackson's hydraulic brake, Clarke's connected brake, Chaplin's electric and the Clark and Webb chain; you got your first automatic vacuum job in 1881, though it wasn't much flaming good and the drivers didn't like it.'

The most prominent sprayed message at Kentish Town was a sombre 'Last Few Days'. At Gospel Oak it was 'Anarchy – The True Way Forward To Free Thought'. The train paused there for only a few seconds and, in the silence, I heard the sound of children playing. The line swung away between comfortable houses standing in substantial gardens. Then, all at once, Hampstead Heath hove into view, a high, rounded hill reaching up to a cloud-dappled skyline. Down by the track there was an adventure playground fashioned from brightly painted timber. The long platforms at Hampstead Heath carried several signs advising, 'Alight here for Royal Free Hospital' – ironically, in view of the eight people crushed to death on the station staircase one bank holiday weekend in 1892 – and one saying, 'Finsbury Park Funk Masters'.

A descending tunnel took us all the way to Finchley Road and Frognal, where there were fine, shady trees by the station and a sign reading, 'Hi Danny'. At West Hampstead, on the wall of a small yellowbrick shed standing by the platform, a more prosaic notice advertised the services of A. J. Phillips, Contractors and Plant For Sale and Hire. Brondesbury had a timber platform and a wooden fence and, through the trees, an array of fine houses. There were brambles and blackberry bushes on the Brondesbury Park platform further down the line; approaching the station, the train ran between beds of vegetables. The run to Kensal Rise was equally brief, taking us past more leafy gardens and roomy houses, giving us a glimpse of a park shot with autumn

A sunny day at Willesden Junction.

159

Willesden Junction ninety years ago. A North London Railway Locomotive can be seen in the top right-hand corner.

colours. At Kensal Rise the covered staircase common to many of these North London stations ascended steeply from the platform ends to a quiet street; my friend told me that one of the North London tank engines built at Bow in 1879 for freight – 'Bleeding rough riders, evidently' – had served on the Cromford and High Peak line in Derbyshire until 1960 and was now preserved by the Bluebell Railway. 'And the North London was the first British railway to introduce coal gas lighting in its carriages,' he added.

Just beyond the Kensal Rise Down platform there was a rabbit hutch containing a huge piebald buck which lifted its upper lip in a sneer as we rattled by. We were going down in the world now, the houses on either side of us growing steadily more nondescript. Willesden was a wasteland of railway tracks and the station itself is split into two – Willesden Low Level and High Level. I said goodbye to my friend, who was going through to Acton, and got off at the High Level, recalling as I looked for the exit that the place was popularly supposed to be thronged with the spirits of people who perished while trying to find the way out.

I had stopped off to meet Mr David Simpson, the Area Manager, a courteous, grey-haired man inhabiting a spartan office in a building down beside the tracks. Looking across the acres of railway lines as we drank tea I asked how many trains went past his window. 'Well, 320 local ones a day for a start,' he said. 'Then there are 130 outer suburban services, 100 freights and 200 express passenger trains in and out of Euston. And 180 freights leave the Willesden freight sidings each week. I have 350 train crews in my area, and last year my cleaning ladies attended to 80,629 coaches and, in season, made 1,000 beds a day on the Euston sleepers.'

As I walked back to catch the next Broad Street service on to Richmond, an Inter-City express passing a few yards away and causing a disturbance like a major earthquake, I reflected that Willesden had not always presented such a bleak and grimy face to the world. A century before, this had been a pretty, prosperous village set in undulating green fields; the local water was so soft and pure that, apart from farming, Willesden's main source of income was its laundries. It had also been a notable religious centre. The ten manors of Willesden-cum-Neasden were once owned by St Paul's Cathedral, where there are still prebendal stalls marked with the names Willesden, Neasden and Harlesden; Willesden's notable prebendaries included William of Wykeham, the bishop who founded both Winchester school and New College, Oxford. There was a Benedictine convent here as well, built on the banks of the Kele-bourne stream (from which the word Kilburn is derived). After Willesden got its first permanent way in 1844 a loop line was laid across the paddocks to leafy Neasden.

Now, setting off for Acton Central over a bridge spanning the great highway of rails linking London with the cities of the north, we moved past the Willesden High Level box and surveyed on the horizon the capital's distant towers and domes. There was a scrapyard soon after the Acton Wells box – the last in a landscape littered with them – and then, all at once, we found ourselves

As the train pulls away from Acton Central, the crossing is opened once more to traffic.

running down a quiet, tree-lined cutting where showers of falling leaves brushed against the windows and there were dandelions in the grass; we could have been travelling along a sleepy Cotswold lane. Acton means 'the farm by the oak trees' and I knew that, in the days when it was just a small village on the Oxford road, the Acton wells enjoyed a brief fashionable flurry as a minor spa. Henry Fielding, the author of *Tom Jones*, lived here, and so did the banker Nathan Rothschild. It was in the library of his home, Gunnersbury House, that he promised Disraeli the money to buy the lease of the Suez Canal.

We trundled on past brambles and plots planted with lettuces. Acton station, handsomely fashioned from pale brick, has fluted chocolate brown columns holding up the platform canopy. At South Acton, there was once a small engine shed, able to accommodate six locomotives. Though the view is impaired by high-rise council flats, South Acton has something of the aura of a country halt, the station garden filled with cabbages and runner beans and lying behind a wooden platform so narrow that the passengers standing on it appeared to suck in their stomachs and hold their breaths as we slid past them to a stop. The tiny waiting room contains a bench as worn and venerable as an old pew.

Down the line at the Bollo Lane box (where the West Kensington coal trains turned off) the signalman was standing on his small wooden balcony, puffing a cigarette and enjoying the hazy afternoon sunshine. A few yards further on we rattled under an abandoned footbridge of mossy, weathered brick with a thick crop of yellowing summer grass growing along its top. Used only by foxes and badgers today, the bridge marks the beginning of the Gunnersbury triangle, central London's only genuine piece of wild woodland. The triangle, a few acres in area, belongs to British Rail and, until 1910, was used for extracting ballast. Then everyone went away and left it alone. In places the diggers had excavated down to the water table and now these marshy areas are filled with black poplar and three species of willow, while the dry parts have yielded forests of silver birches. There are families of foxes in residence and, at sunrise, herons flap in to breakfast off the little green frogs in the marsh. In the spring it is carpeted with wildflowers.

At the foot of the triangle, beneath the London Transport Research Laboratory, the train swings right and clatters across a set of points to join the District Line and the Underground system. Gunnersbury station is only a moment or two beyond the junction, but it is a sombre place, the platforms flanked by concrete car parks and lying in the shadow of the towering IBM building. The train crosses the Thames on a sturdy iron bridge, passing the elegant new Public Records Office almost as soon as it arrives on the south bank. Kew Gardens station, obsessively neat and well-kept, has a smart buffet on the Up platform and on the Down a pair of half-timbered Wendy houses, one the premises of the Lea Valley Florists, the other of A. C. Tompkins, a broker of businesses.

On the final sector I looked out at a pair of gasometers, a timber yard, the Avenue Engraving Works, a yard full of ancient buses and then, at the entrance to the station, Richmond's curious ark-shaped signal box. The Broad Street train usually ends its journey at platform seven, the passengers hurrying off past faded advertisements for the Red Lion Chinese restaurant and the Richmond Bookshop – 'Art, Music, Poetry, Philosophy, Psychology, Literary Criticism and Biography, Libraries Purchased'. A District Line train had just drawn up at platform six and the driver, an earnest young man with a slight limp, headed away clutching a samovar-sized pot which he clearly intended to fill with tea.

Before leaving the train I paused for a moment to chat to the guard. He told me that until 1921 the North London (in common with most lines) did not run on Sunday mornings during the hours of Divine Service. He also said that the world's first train murder took place on the line. 'A bloke called Thomas Briggs was stabbed to death in a North London first class compartment in 1864. We had another murder half a century after that, some geezer killed just after the train had pulled out of Broad Street. And then in 1899 a French governess strangled her illegitimate kid and left him in the waiting room at Dalston Junction.'